GREAT REJECTS

DESIGN THAT

PROVES SECOND

CHOICE ISN'T

SECOND BEST

ROCKPORT
PUBLISHERS

Rockport Publishers, Rockport, Massachusetts

Distributed by
North Light Books, Cincinnati, Ohio

First published in the United States of America by:
Rockport Publishers
146 Granite Street
Rockport, Massachusetts 01966
Telephone: (508) 546-9590
Fax: (508) 546-7141

Distributed to the book and art trades in the U.S. by:
North Light, an imprint of
F & W Publications
1507 Dana Avenue
Cincinnati, Ohio 45207
Telephone: (513) 531-2222

Other distribution by:
Rockport Publishers, Inc.
Rockport, Massachusetts 01966

ISBN 1-56496-205-9

10 9 8 7 6 5 4 3 2 1

Produced by:
Supon Design Group, International Book Division
1700 K Street, NW, Suite 400
Washington, DC 20006
Telephone: (202) 822-6540
Fax: (202) 822-6541

Project and Art Director: Supon Phornirunlit
Managing Editor: Wayne Kurie
Writers: Linda Klinger, Wayne Kurie
Editors: Christina Doykos, Shawna Mullen
Book Jacket Designer: Heather Yale
Book Jacket Images: Front cover: pp. 74 and 75
                    Back cover (left to right): pp. 133 and 71
Book Interior Designer: Richard Law
Production: Beth Santos Design

Special thanks to all those who made this book possible, including Henry Kornman of HK Marketing Service, and Winnie Danenbarger, Rosalie Grattaroti, and G. Stanley Patey of Rockport Publishers, Inc.

Printed in Hong Kong by Regent Publishing Services Limited

TABLE OF CONTENTS

INTRODUCTION

Here are a few things that this book is not: It's not a compilation of failures. It's not about incompetency or inadequacy in commercial art. And it certainly does not tout deficiencies in the world of design.

This is a book about great rejects—cast-offs, indeed, but placed in the positive, educational context that first-rate works deserve. This is a collection of unrealized, exceptionally good work—but mostly unpublished and even abandoned by its creators. It is our hope that, with this recognition, the significance of these works in the world of design is newly resurrected.

The contents of this publication came from a variety of sources and situations. Most often, these rejects resulted from a design firm's presentation where multiple comps were shown to a client. Rather than concentrating on the concept selected, we highlight those choices not approved. Some clients will not commit to a single design firm and invite many contributions to ensure a vast cross-section of material; but, by doing so, they accept only one solution and reject the work of several firms altogether. We've displayed the outstanding work of the overlooked studios. Or, as another example, four design firms may have bid on a single project; we show the pieces not chosen.

What's the benefit in this? Neil Steinberg, in his book celebrating runners-up and alternates, summarized it accurately: "The second-placers and also-rans [are] sometimes better, more interesting, even more worthy, than those whose combination of luck, effort, and circumstance for some reason brought success."

The second-placers you'll find here are highly original, and some are even ingenious. They are valuable both because of what they offer and what they don't, when compared to the single work that was chosen. Often these pieces were rejected not because they were less valid or less adept at solving the problem, but because of the subjectivity of the chooser—a variable over which designers have no control.

These rejects offer the reader another perspective or two; they stretch the client's former perception of the way he/she sees the organization or service illustrated, and how well the designer captured the essence of it. The pieces are all worthy, but perhaps they followed a muse in an undesired direction—one contrary to the client's whims. They are valid, but perhaps the client's personal preference rebelled against the color blue. The work chosen may not have been a better solution, but simply in the right place, at the right time. In fact, the client may have chosen the less creative work to avoid conflicts with a company's established comfort zone.

So, rather than letting these rejects pass into obscurity without recognition, we have gathered them here and given them a phoenix-like opportunity for rebirth.

Rejection is an integral part of the creative process of any artistic venture, and it is necessary for the designer to undergo it, to create when the concept is unwieldy and vague, and emerge on the other side of the process. Perhaps the designer will emerge successful, but undoubtedly he or she will at minimum acquire the advantage of experience. Those whose livelihood includes creativity, in fact, should embrace the losses. In life, says Russian poet and novelist Boris Pasternak, it is more necessary to lose than to gain. The suspension of the ego is paramount, however; having one's work rejected cannot be regarded as a personal affront.

We chose some of the best works from around the world for inclusion in this collection of work that has been undeservingly cast off. The approaches for many of the solutions are appropriate and highly creative. All of them address their problems exceptionally well. They also do something else—they demonstrate the process by which designers create; the evolution of solutions from one to the next is inspiring. And the way each work blazes its own trail of distinction is a constant source of interest for novice and experienced designers alike.

It is the designer's responsibility to not only address the objectives of the project—to portray the client in a unique and marketable way—but to put order to the imprecise concept. Thankfully, there are many ways to do this, each solution deviating more from the expected than the last. In fact, one hopes all the possibilities present entirely different approaches.

This book was born out of the misplaced praise we often attribute to the "winners." Yet we are not trying to discredit those leaders—they're obviously good, or they wouldn't be successful. We hope readers will instead gain a sensibility for the value of the discarded.

Maybe it's not so bad to be second. And books like this one prove that nobody loses all of the time.

GREAT SELECTS

Here, in addition to solutions rejected by the client, you'll also find those that were accepted.

There is a unique story behind the reasons for each choice. Perhaps, for example, the design ultimately chosen establishes an entirely new direction, one that doesn't match previous attempts depicted and instead moves the client into a different dimension. Sometimes the final design combines elements from other solutions. The design approved may simply provide a "safer," more conservative, or more comfortable style—one with which the client is familiar.

The range of approaches used by a single design firm in its attempt to address the client's interest can be astounding. As in a great recipe, that one missing, intangible ingredient that answers the client need is eventually added, producing the winning combination. Designers or readers may not always agree with the client's choice—stronger designs or those that better convey a message can be passed over for reasons that are not clear. But all works included here share one commonality: they are all excellent, and all deserve a second look.

JOEL CONFER SOFTBALL TEAM LOGO

Task

Design a distinctive mark for a softball team's uniform shirts.

Design Strategies

The rejected design was intended to simulate, through the use of type, a playing field with players and balls. The clients, however, did not recognize the softball elements and felt the design was too plain. The final choice resembled a favorite Big League team. To address team concerns about too much ink on the shirt, which would retain heat, the application was changed from a two-color design on the chest to a smaller, one-color version over the pocket.

Design Firm: Sommese Design
Client: Joel Confer Softball Team
Art Director: Lanny Sommese
Designers: Lanny Sommese, Jenn Miller

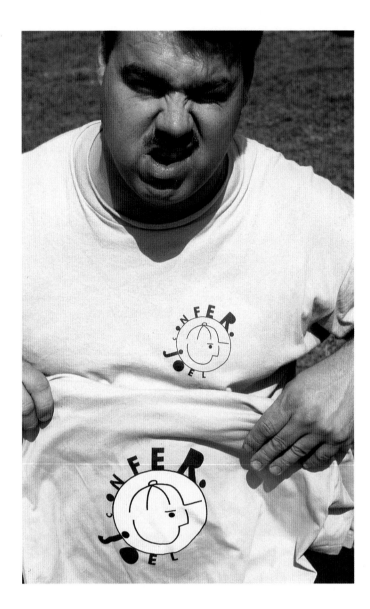

LAUGH AMERICA LOGO

Task

Create an identity for a new line of funny, satirical greeting cards.

Design Strategies

The accepted solution was originally based on the Groucho nose/glasses/moustache look. The designers' favorite was influenced by Looney Tunes and simulated sound effects associated with comic strips (note word balloon for "Greetings"). Another touted the relationship of "H" and "A," and the visuals communicated the satirical nature of the cards. At top is one of a series of classic comedy situations; others included a person slipping on a banana peel and a cream pie battle.

Design Firm: Laughing Dog Creative, Inc.
Client: Recycled Paper Greetings, Inc.
Art Director: Frank EE Grubich
Designers: Tim Meyer, Frank EE Grubich

WOLF TRAP CAMPAIGN

Task

Create a campaign for a theater for the performing arts.

Design Strategies

To convey spring and summer—Wolf Trap's high season—warm-toned hues were chosen. The designers emphasized the client's variety of outstanding music, dance, and theater events with a look that was playful and gay. The chosen solution used colors and icons that transferred easily to different applications and smaller sizes. Some figures were turned into spot icons and used throughout the campaign.

Design Firm: Supon Design Group
Client: Wolf Trap Center for the
    Performing Arts
Art Director: Supon Phornirunlit
Designer and Illustrator: Steve Morris

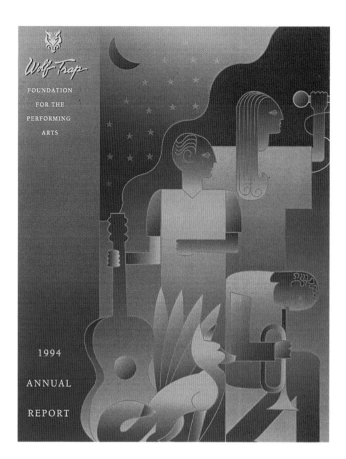

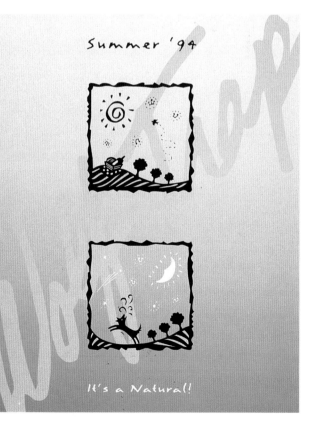

FRANK RUSSELL LIFE-POINTS BROCHURE

Task

Create a range of materials to support a new 401(k) program for an institutional investment company.

Design Strategies

The design addressed two plans: Participant (for individual employees or users) and Sponsorship (for corporate administration officers). The rejected versions provided a framework for developing the friendly, approachable collateral system that was later accepted. Large type treatments alleviate the intimidating print frequently found in financial material. Warm illustrations lighten up factual information and color headlines break up data into digestible portions. Tabbing and color coding make the material easier to understand.

Design Firm: Hornall Anderson Design Works, Inc.
Client: The Frank Russell Company
Art Director: Jack Anderson
Designers: Jack Anderson, Lisa Cerveny, Suzanne Haddon
Illustrator: Julia LaPine
Photographer: John Still

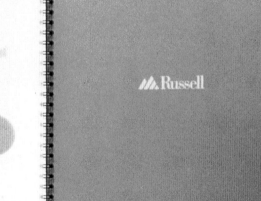

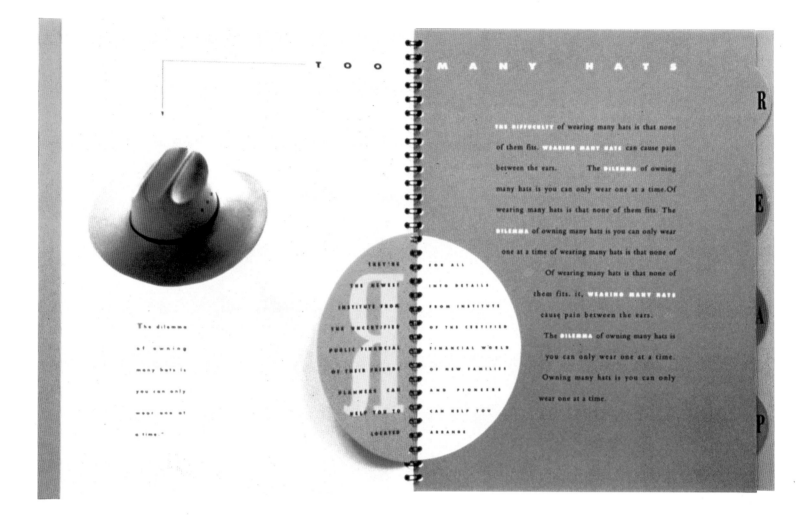

T O O   M A N Y   H A T S

THE DIFFICULTY of wearing many hats is that none of them fits. WEARING MANY HATS can cause pain between the ears.   The DILEMMA of owning many hats is you can only wear one at a time. Of wearing many hats is that none of them fits. The DILEMMA of owning many hats is you can only wear one at a time of wearing many hats is that none of Of wearing many hats is that none of them fits. it, WEARING MANY HATS cause pain between the ears. The DILEMMA of owning many hats is you can only wear one at a time. Owning many hats is you can only wear one at a time.

The dilemma of owning many hats is you can only wear one at a time.

THEY'RE   FOR ALL
THE NEWEST   INTO DETAILS
INSTITUTE FROM FROM INSTITUTE
THE UNCERTIFIED OF THE CERTIFIED
PUBLIC FINANCIAL FINANCIAL WORLD
OF THEIR FRIENDS OF NEW FAMILIES
PLANNERS CAN   AND PIONEERS
HELP YOU TO   CAN HELP YOU
LOCATED   ARRANGE

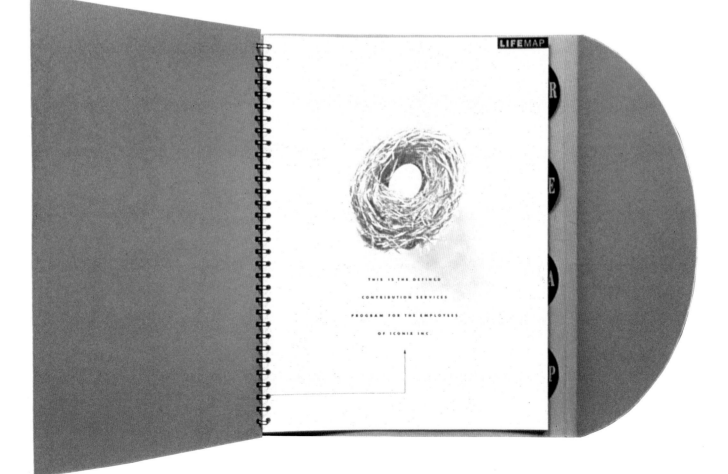

LIFEMAP

THIS IS THE DEFINED
CONTRIBUTION SERVICES
PROGRAM FOR THE EMPLOYEES
OF ICONIX INC.

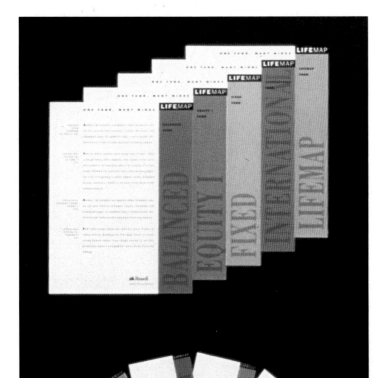

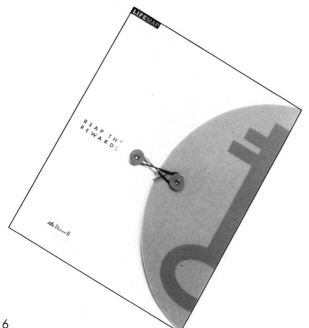

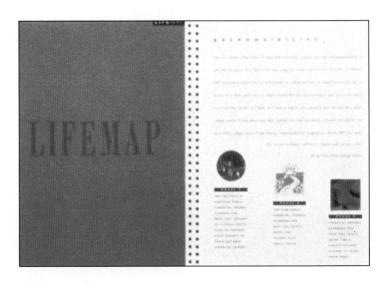

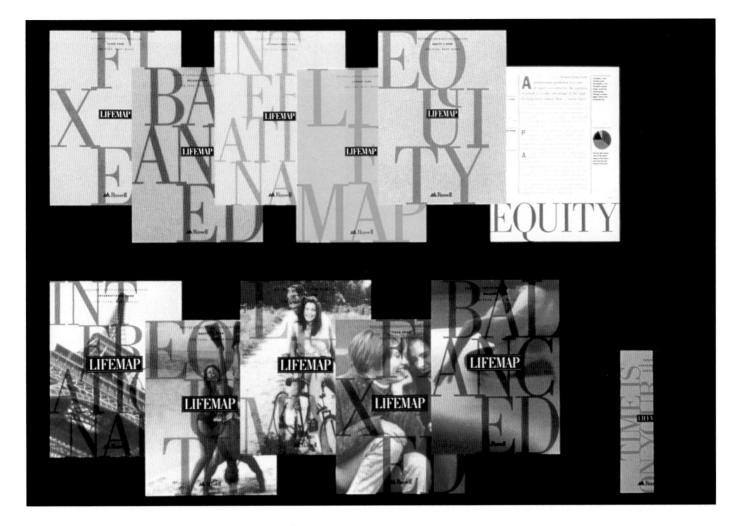

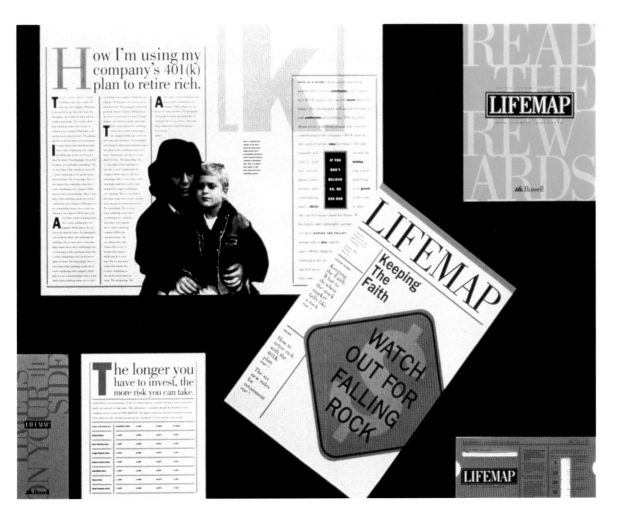

CLEMENTE JACQUES SALSA PICANTE PACKAGING

Task

Elevate the consumer's perception and increase usage of this line of salsa products.

Design Strategies

Having long been a popular brand in its native Mexico, Clemente Jacques is a *salsa auténtica*. The designers wanted to illustrate this benefit with colorful art suggestive of its heritage. But to appeal to the American market, they also wanted to mold the perception of the product as a condiment appropriate for all dishes, not just Mexican. The client, however, preferred a more straightforward design—one more consistent with the brand's original Mexican label.

Design Firm: Wallace Church Associates
Client: Van Den Bergh Foods Company,
    Unilever's Food Division
Art Director: Stan Church
Designer: Joe Cuticone
Illustrator: Karen Kluglein

HCC ANNUAL
REPORT

Task

Design an annual report oriented towards the future plans of a company in transition.

Design Strategies

Capitalizing on the fact that the client would soon provide greater control over health care–related costs through computer links, one rejected layout used light and color in a unique way to emphasize this energy and forward thought, avoiding the clichéd, "high-tech" look. The soft colors emphasizing user-friendliness was the concept chosen and executed.

Design Firm: Laughing Dog Creative, Inc.
Client: HealthCare COMPARE Corp.
Art Director and Designer:
   Frank EE Grubich
Photographer: Pierre-Yves Goavec

MQM PROGRAM

Task
Create a look for a new program focusing on quality and management's new direction called "McDonald's Quality Management."

Design Strategies
Using the program's intent of getting "back to basics," the client's uncomplicated but forward-thinking communication goals were illustrated using a cup-and-string visual (with client soft drink cups). This concept was rejected because the client feared it would look too expensive to upper management. The approved direction highlighted the program's simplicity with large type, primary colors, and graphic faces. Ironically, the chosen concept was just as expensive to produce as the rejected one.

Design Firm: Laughing Dog Creative, Inc.
Client: McDonald's
Art Director: Frank EE Grubich
Designer: Tim Meyer
Photographer: David Rigg Photography

NUTELLA PACKAGING AND IDENTITY DESIGN

Task
Transform the brand identity of this European hazelnut and cocoa spread to that of an all-American product.

Design Strategies
Because of its chocolate content, Americans have tended to view Nutella as a dessert topping. The many different label comps which the designers presented were meant to change this perception, i.e., to portray the product as appropriate for consumption any time of day. Illustrations showed the spread on foods as diverse as strawberries and oranges, crackers, breads, and croissants. Even the treatment of the Nutella name was altered—sometimes slightly, sometimes more radically—in hopes of appealing to the American market's distinct tastes. In the end, however, the client was averse to too much of a departure from its already entrenched global identity and requested a portrayal closer to that of the original.

Design Firm: Wallace Church Associates
Client: Ferrero
Art Director: Stan Church
Designers: John Waski, Wendy Church, Christine Cambell
Illustrator: Matthew Holmes

CYBER PRODUCTIONS LOGO

Task

Design an identity for a start-up company that produces interactive multimedia presentations for businesses.

Design Strategies

To give this client a strong, established look, several approaches were proposed, including an eye form with a monitor screen shape; type treatment bookended by "circuit board" brackets; a human form interacting with electronics, visuals, and sound; and other visual links between persons and the mechanics of multimedia. The accepted logo used a human head to represent the interactive dimension of multimedia, and wedge-shaped mouth, eyes, and ears to show the flow of visual and audio information.

Design Firm: Joseph Rattan Design
Client: Cyber Productions
Art Director: Joseph Rattan
Designers: Greg Morgan, Joseph Rattan

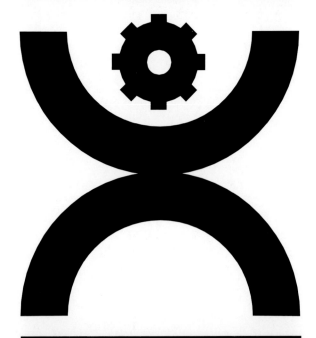

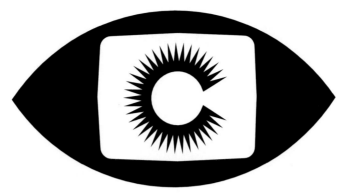

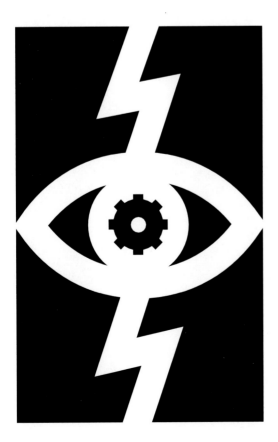

NEW IMAGE FASHION IDENTITY

Task

Design an identity for a small fashion boutique specializing in computer-assisted makeovers.

Design Strategies

The project's main objective was to create a bold image that emphasized two components: the face, and the link between the computer imaging process and the application of different hairstyles and makeup. The alternate design, a more stylized impression of these components, was rejected by the client, who felt the realistic image with applied graphic treatments was more appropriate.

Design Firm: Burton Nesbitt Graphic Design
Client: New Image Fashion Boutique
Art Director: Burton Nesbitt Graphic Design
Designers: Kelly Burton, Roger Nesbitt

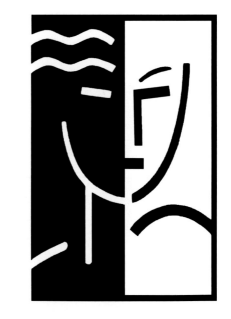

NEW IMAGE
fashion

K2 SKIS
(8.3 SLC RACE)

Task
Design a fashion-inspired ski that appeals to both retailers and competitive skiers.

Design Strategies
To promote this ski, it was important to balance fashion with performance and function. The initial race ski was designed with bold, rainbow colors on a white background. Retailers rejected this one because it lacked the K2 logo chain—preferred by race skiers, as it contrasted from more recreational, fashion-statement skis. The revised version contained a black background with subtle red and purple graphics and incorporated the K2 logo.

Design Firm: Hornall Anderson Design
    Works, Inc.
Client: K2 Corporation
Art Director: Jack Anderson
Designers: Jack Anderson, Mary Hermes,
    David Bates, John Anicker,
    Brian O'Neill

FARMER DIRECT PACKAGING

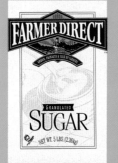

Task
Create a flexible, but unifying, package design system and apply it to other "commodity" products sold under the Farmer Direct name.

Design Strategies
Farmer Direct is a consortium of growers who sell their products directly to retailers, thus eliminating the middleman and assuring fresher produce. Therefore, a strong association between the brand name and an image of locally grown, farm-freshness inspired the concepts of all presented designs. The final design of the flour label was adapted to fit other Farmer Direct products, optimizing shelf presence.

Design Firm: Wallace Church Associates
Client: American Crystal Sugar
Art Director: Stan Church
Designer: John Waski
Illustrator: Mark Riedy

ALL-PURPOSE
Flour

ENRICHED·PRESIFTED·BLEACHED

NET WT.5 LB(2.26kg)

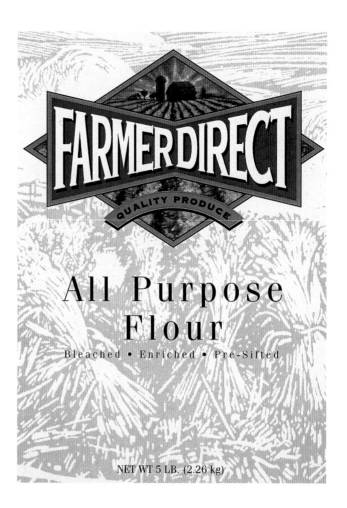

ALL-PURPOSE

FLOUR

Bleached-Enriched-Presifted

Net Wt. 5 LB.(2.26 Kg)

ALL-PURPOSE

FLOUR

NET WT.5 LB.(226kg)

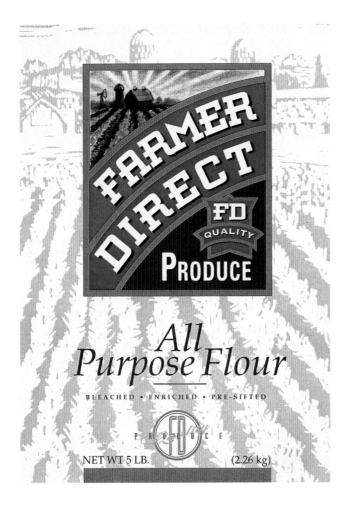

All
Purpose Flour

BLEACHED · ENRICHED · PRE-SIFTED

NET WT 5 LB.   (2.26 kg)

ALL-PURPOSE

FLOUR

ENRICHED-PRESIFTED-BLEACHED

NET WT.5 LB.(2.26kg)

THE UNDERNEATH MOVIE POSTER

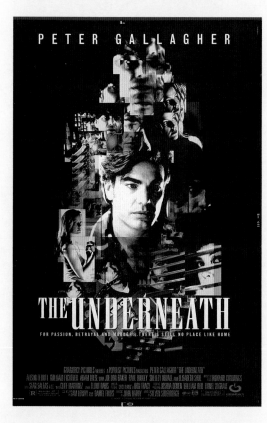

Task

Design a poster showing the many facets of a story in a contemporary style.

Design Strategies

Research showed moviegoers respond to posters that are oblique in their message and modern in their look. The client requested a cool but cryptic design. To add a new dimension to the main ingredient in the picture—actor Peter Gallagher—the designers broke his facial image into cubes and floated it over a Daliesque landscape with graphic elements that hinted at the story line—guns, money, an armored car. The chosen design was a less radical execution of this many-faceted look.

Design Firm: Mike Salisbury
    Communications, Inc.
Client: Gramercy Pictures
Art Director: Samantha Hart
Designer: Mike Salisbury
Illustrator: Ron Brown

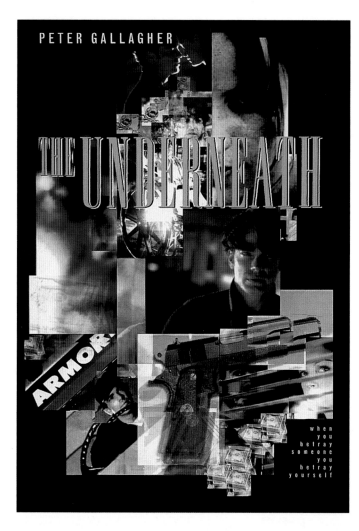

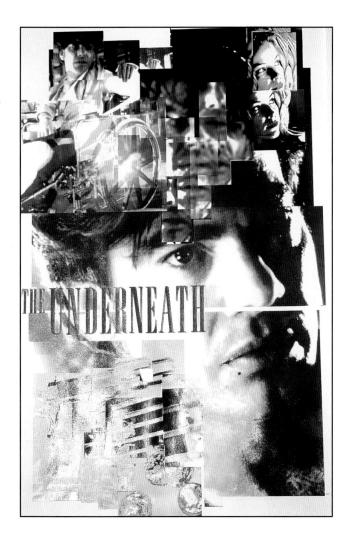

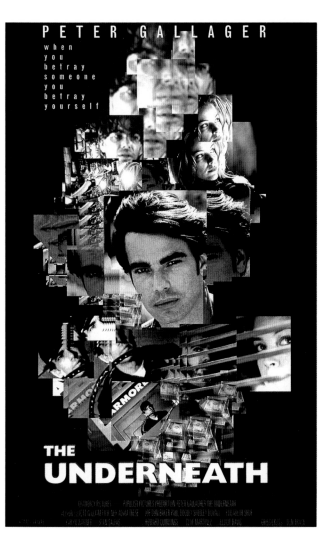

TASTE OF THE NATION LOGO

Task

Create a logo to represent Montreal's event in a gala celebration.

Design Strategies

The objective was to convey the idea of giving and sharing both spiritually (i.e., heart and soul) and physically (food). Because the event centered on free participation, costs had to be cut at all levels. The serene face represented in the plate in the chosen solution depicts a sense of caring. The designers personally preferred a stronger illustration, however, featured in hand and heart elements.

Design Firm: Graffiti Parc Design
Client: American Express Taste of the
   Nation Gala
Art Director and Designer: Laurence Parc

taste of the nation

table du partage

TASTE OF THE NATION

TABLE DU PARTAGE

taste of the nation

Taste of the Nation

Table du Partage

HEWLETT PACKARD PACKAGING

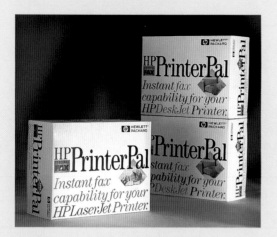

Task

Design new packaging for the client's entire line of printers and accessories using the client's corporate design standards as guidelines.

Design Strategies

To effectively present a "why to buy" message, the designers developed new packaging graphics with a "billboard" panel, which was accepted by the client. The designers recommended a customized UPC bar code as well, but this was not implemented. Within a year, however, the client's corporate design standards were set aside, and the studio's new packaging design was accepted and produced for the retail marketplace.

Design Firm: THARP AND DRUMMOND
   DID IT
Client: Hewlett-Packard
Art Directors: Rick Tharp,
   Charles Drummond
Designers: Dean Estes, Jana Heer,
   Laurie Okamura, Randy Stepon,
Colleen Sullivan, Rick Tharp
Copywriter: Charles Drummond
Product Managers: Carrie Strader,
   Pat Deaner, Ron Provencio

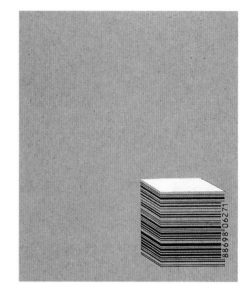

STOLAS GROUP LOGO

Task
Design a logo for a small company that develops medical patient tracking and accounting software.

Design Strategies
Several of the proposed designs worked with the caduceus as a visual icon, which indicated a high-tech medical firm. Though a somewhat clichéd icon, the non-typical choice of pastel colors strengthened these designs. Other possibilities included an elegant, opposing blend with a graceful vertical visual movement; and the designers' preference—a combination of the pastels the client favored in a strong visual using the "S" and "G" initials. The client, however, felt it wasn't bold enough. They chose the "friendly" script design instead.

Design Firm: Shields Design
Client: The Stolas Group
Art Director: Charles Shields
Designers: Charles Shields, Laura Thornton

ARTS ALIVE
LOGO

ARTS
ALIVE

Task
Create a logo for an art series.

Design Strategies
The mark had to represent several different art events held over a period of a month, and also function in one color. The proposed solutions used implied movements to affect a variety of elegant or eclectic elements. The client chose the classic serif "A" because of its more conservative style, which contrasted with the flourish of the "C."

Design Firm: Trudy Cole-Zielanski Design
Client: Frostburg State University
Art Director, Designer, and Illustrator:
    Trudy Cole-Zielanski

[ARTS ALIVE]

ARTS ALIVE

ARTS ALIVE

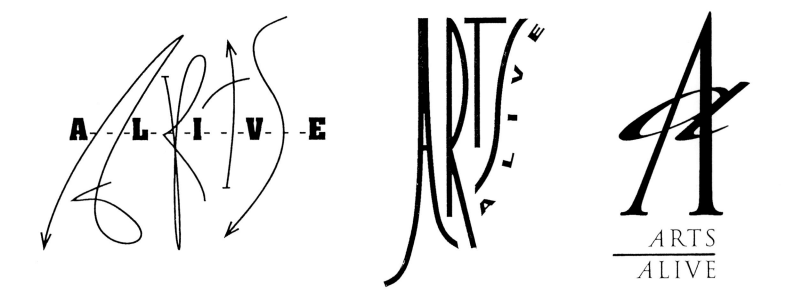

A·L·I·V·E

ARTS
ALIVE

arts alive

[ARTS ALIVE]

arts alive

FLEXOLOGY COLLATERAL

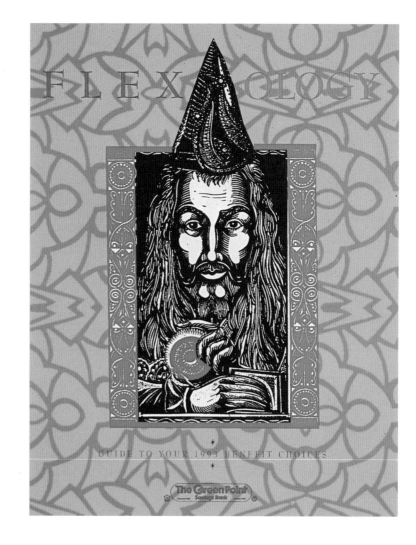

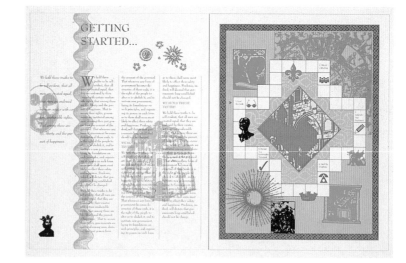

Task

Design an internal communication piece for an employee benefits program.

Design Strategies

The designers attempted to visually enhance material that is often tedious to read by using a wise and whimsical spokesman—the wizard—and playing up his experience rather than his magical skills. Each program element used a different woodcut pattern to reflect the medieval times. The client, however, felt this approach was too sophisticated. Accompanying illustrations prevented the selected design from resembling a cartoon.

Design Firm: Toni Schowalter Design
Client: Greenpoint Savings Bank
Art Director: Toni Schowalter
Designers: Toni Schowalter, Ilene Price
Illustrators: Stephen Alcorn, Alex Murawski

FLEXOLOGY

★

GUIDE TO YOUR 1993

★

BENEFIT CHOICES

★

THE GREENPOINT SAVINGS BANK

FLEX-
OLOGY

★

HIGHLIGHTS OF

★

YOUR 1993

★

BENEFIT CHOICES

★

THE GREENPOINT SAVINGS BANK

39

MISSIVE LOGO

MISSIVE

Task

Develop an image/icon for a new computer messaging software.

Design Strategies

In an effort to create strong, stark, and simple designs for a busy, complex product, two concepts produced multiple solutions. The first was the "big-bang" concept, which illustrated central, stabilizing forces that routed incoming and outgoing messages of various formats. The second was the "chaos" concept, which portrayed the software as a means of creating order. The client responded positively to all logos presented, but felt they may compete too much with the existing corporate identity, and opted to use a typographic solution instead.

Design Firm: Planet Design Company
Client: Wingra Technologies
Art Directors: Dana Lytle, Kevin Wade
Designers: Dana Lytle, Kevin Wade,
   Martha Graettinger

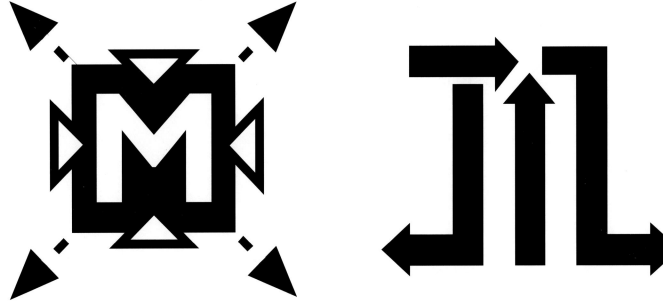

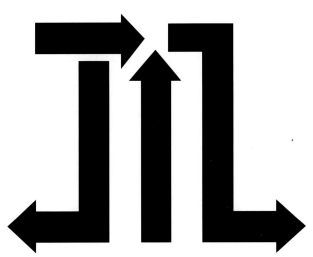

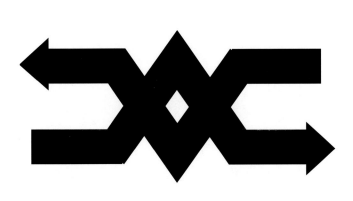

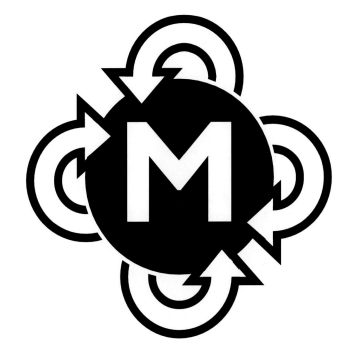

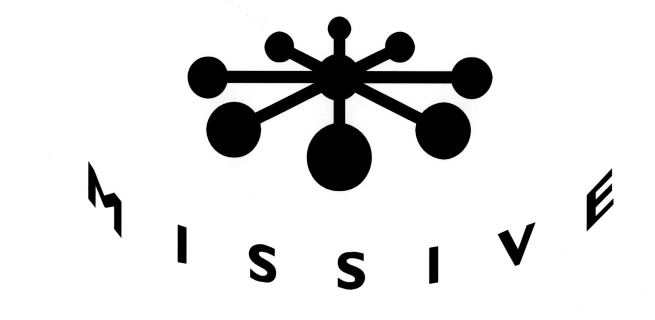

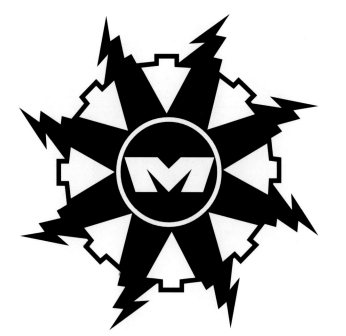

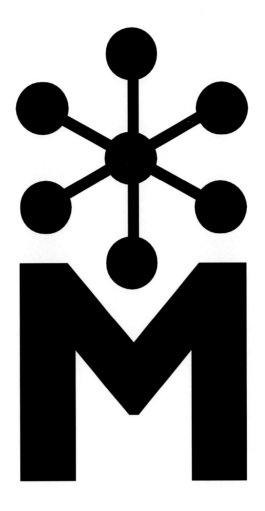

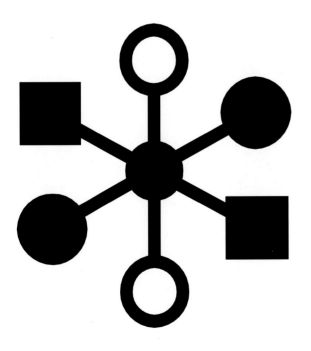

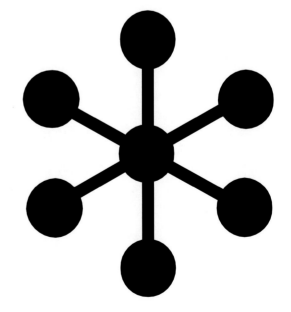

FRUIT SHOCKER PACKAGING

Task

Design a package for a soft-frozen, fruit-flavored drink.

Design Strategies

With limited colors, the designers displayed the "fun" aspect of the product through a visual of a person whose hair is standing on end, drinking the beverage. But this was seen as too youthful. Another solution highlighted just the lemon, as the client hadn't yet decided to offer any other flavors. The client liked the design's simplicity, but felt it would eventually be limiting. The solution that incorporated many fruits in a geometric style was a finalist, but lacked the fun attitude they were looking for. The final design was selected because of its "cut-paper" illustration which communicated "fun and fruity" to a wide age group.

Design Firm: John Evans Design
Client: Bassham Foods
Art Director, Designer, and Illustrator:
   John Evans

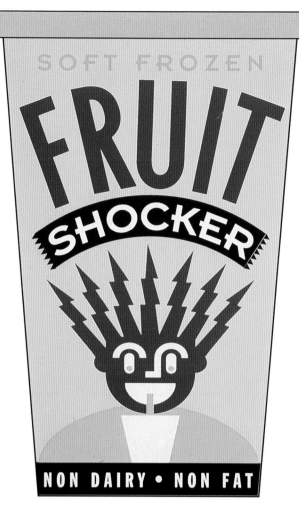

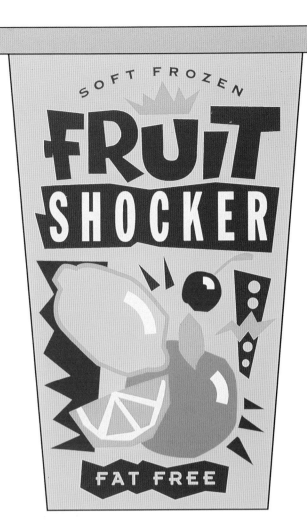

SOFT FROZEN
FRUiT
SHOCKER

FAT FREE

SOFT FROZEN
FRUIT
SHOCKER

100% NATURAL

SOFT FROZEN

FRUIT
SHOCKER

100% NATURAL

SOFT FROZEN
FRUIT
SHOCKER

CENTER FOR CORPORATE LEARNING BROCHURE

Task

Design a corporate brochure for a learning center that would be a source of employee information, training, and counseling.

Design Strategies

The rejected concept read like a museum guide—a non-linear approach that could be understood from whatever point the reader started. Each spread was designed to be a complete thought, and the slick brochure would emphasize the Center's wide range of programs. The accepted solution was a link to the client's overall "back to basics" theme, using an uncomplicated folded, single-sheet style with photos of simple wooden items.

Design Firm: Laughing Dog Creative, Inc.
Client: McDonald's
Art Director: Frank EE Grubich
Designer: Frank EE Grubich

TECHMONTH IDENTITY

Task

Design a corporate identity program for an annual event which focuses on technology for one month.

Design Strategies

To create a design that could be used again from year to year, several approaches were attempted, most using variations of the oval shape. The client showed a preference for incorporating type in the solution rather than using just a symbol; "Tec Month" and the somewhat long-winded "National Science & Technology Month" were proposed. The mark ultimately chosen coined "Techmonth," which emphasized the word "Tech" and better reflected the technology theme.

Design Firm: Design Objectives Pte Ltd
Client: National Science & Technology Board
Art Director and Designer: Ronnie S.C. Tan

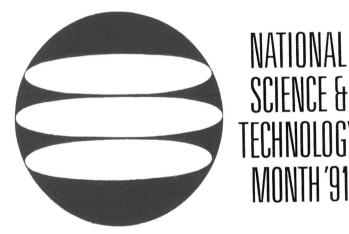

INTEL MATH COPROCESSOR PACKAGING

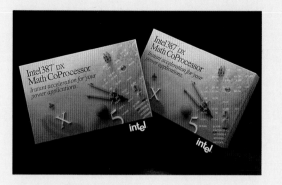

Task

Design that supports Intel's product and market position as a leader in the software category.

Design Strategies

The client wanted to convey a more humanized look versus the high-tech grids and arrows used on previous packaging. The design concept used warm, still-life photos integrated with recognizable math icons, and started with black-and-white layouts, later evolving to colored, three-dimensional studies. The collage approach consisted of various tools used in math processing. The final design was chosen due to its contrasting warmth when compared to the cold, technical appearance of the first design studies.

Design Firm: Hornall Anderson Design
   Works, Inc.
Client: Intel Corporation
Art Directors: Jack Anderson, Julia LaPine
Designers: Jack Anderson, Julia LaPine,
   Denise Weir, David Bates

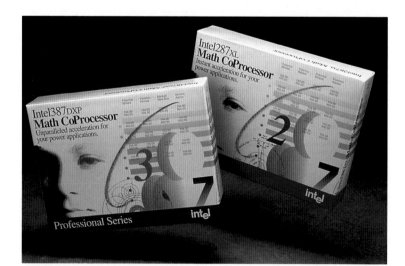

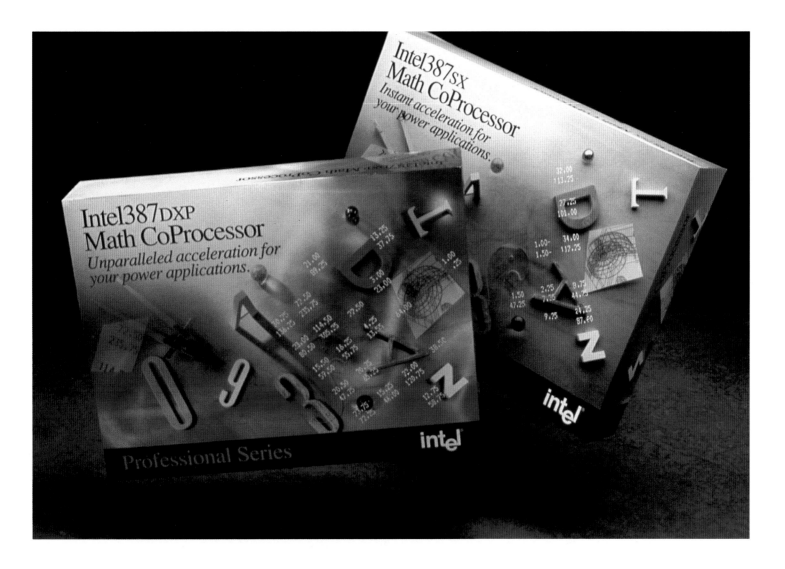

Intel Math CoProcessor
Professional Series
The ultimate accelerator for your power applications.

4

i387DXP

intel

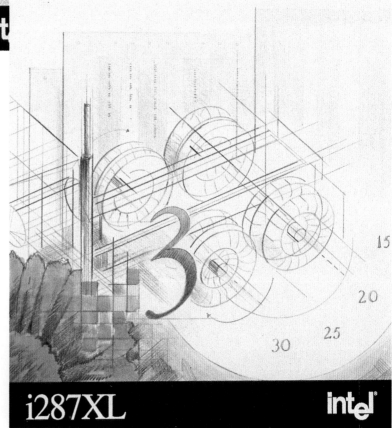

Intel Math CoProcessor
Speeds up your power applications.

3

i287XL

intel

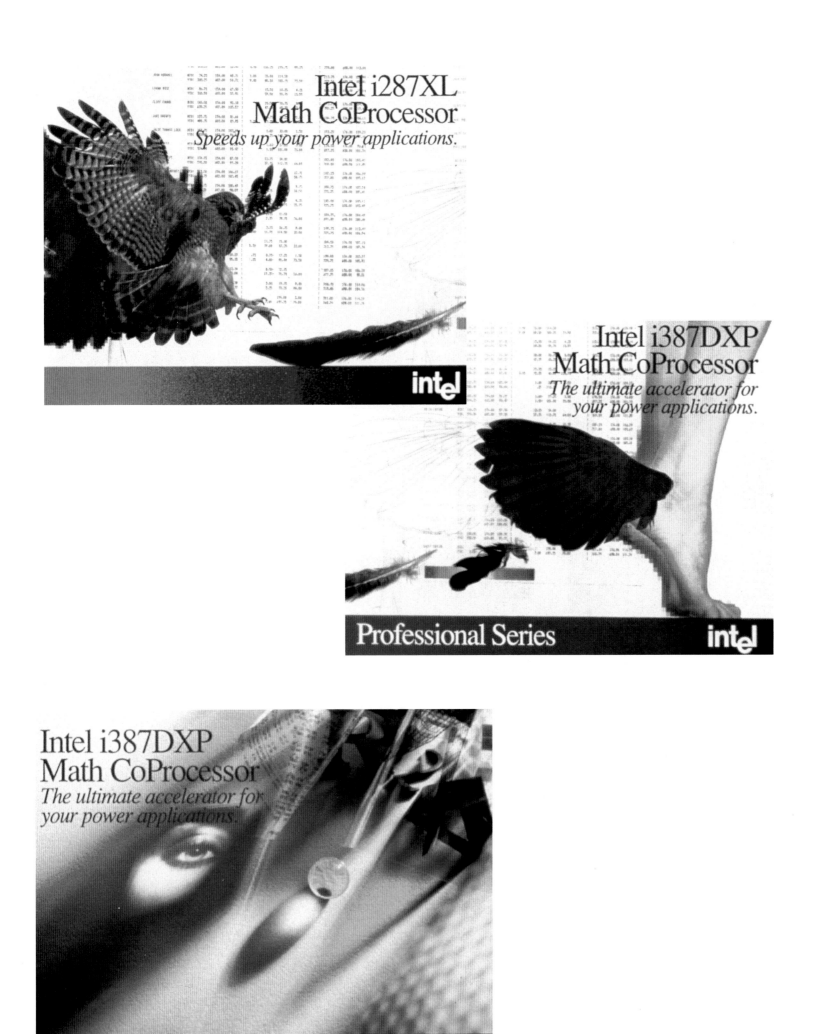

Intel i387DXP
Math CoProcessor

The ultimate accelerator for your power applications.

Professional Series

Intel i287XL
Math CoProcessor

Speeds up your power applications.

Intel Math CoProcessor
Speeds up your power applications.

i287XL

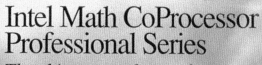

**Intel Math CoProcessor
Professional Series**
*The ultimate accelerator for
your power applications.*

i387DXP

intel

**Intel Math CoProcessor
Professional Series**
*The ultimate accelerator for
your power applications.*

i387DXP

intel

XINET
SOFTWARE
PACKAGING

Task

Design a CD–ROM package for a Macintosh/UNIX server software program.

Design Strategies

The design had to accomplish several objectives: stand out in a retail environment as well as on the user's shelf; communicate the product's function and versatility; and incorporate multiple product benefits. The client chose the metaphor of a server managing two computers, with a typographic pattern of product benefits.

Design Firm: Earl Gee Design
Client: Xinet, Inc.
Art Directors: Earl Gee, Fani Chung
Designers: Earl Gee, Fani Chung
Illustrator: Robert Pastrana
Production: Adrian Fernandez

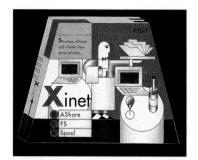

CLARIS
CLEAR CHOICE
SOFTWARE
PACKAGING LINE

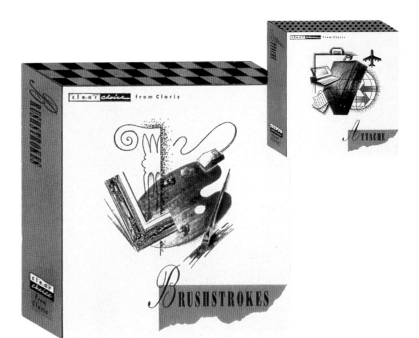

Task

Design packaging for a line of affordably priced personal and productivity software.

Design Strategies

For high shelf impact and to be distinctive across a product line and multiple platforms, bold, graphic representations were used for all solutions, with a heroic sense of scale to symbolize the "power" of the client's applications. The client's choice used strong colors, patterns, and symbolic icons to differentiate products within the line and encourage impulse buying.

Design Firm: Earl Gee Design
Client: Claris Clear Choice
Art Director: Earl Gee
Designers: Earl Gee, Fani Chung
Illustrators: Earl Gee, David Bottoms

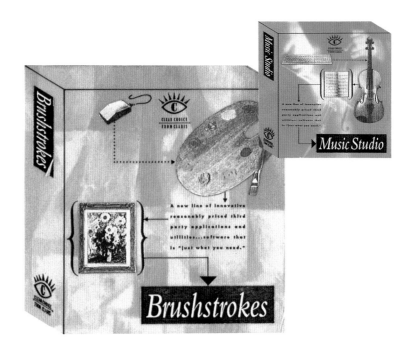

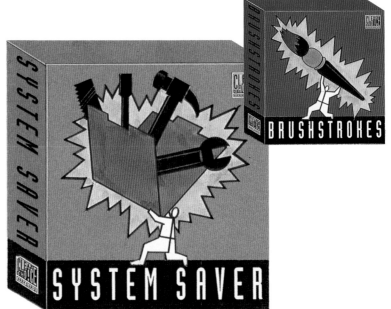

CANADA
A PORTRAIT
BOOK
DUST JACKET

Task

Design a new dust jacket using existing title typography.

Design Strategies

Although the client indicated a preference for a photograph on the cover, the designer offered a variety of concepts. Interestingly, those solutions based on a photographic approach were rejected first. The paintings received positive feedback, as they addressed the need to relate to people of all ages, and also competed successfully with the numerous small informational books available across Canada. The final choice was a contemporary landscape painting. The designer's preference was the white cover, however, because of its graphic strength and shelf presence.

Design Firm: Neville Smith Graphic Design
Client: Statistics Canada
Art Director and Designer: Neville Smith
Illustrators: Neville Smith, Frank Mayrs

57

ROBERT BROWN SCOTCH PACKAGING

Task
Repackage a domestic brand of Japanese scotch to successfully compete with imported labels.

Design Strategies
Traditional looks for this category of liquor bottles were developed, but emphasized styles and approaches that the Japanese did not often use, including the selected design, which featured an authentic Celtic print as a border motif.

Design Firm: Mike Salisbury
    Communications, Inc.
Client: Kirin Breweries and Distilleries
Art Director and Designer: Mike Salisbury
Illustrator: Pat Linse
Lettering: Brian Sisson

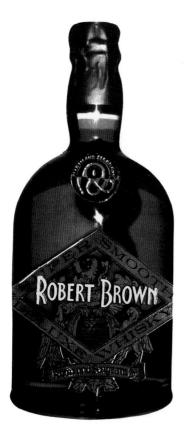

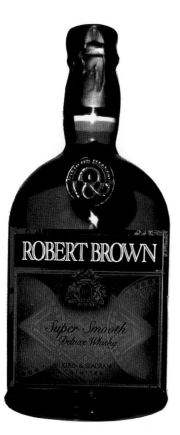

PHILMAC
CORPORATE TIES

Task
Create a design encouraging a wide range of staff members to wear a corporate tie.

Design Strategies
The objective of the design firm was to present a fresh, informal image that incorporated the company logotype and corporate colors. The tie needed to work well for everyday use as well as after-hours occasions. Although the client liked the results of the rejected version, they accepted the more plain corporate tie, which included Australia's national colors, yellow and green.

Design Firm: Burton Nesbitt Graphic Design
Client: Philmac Pty Ltd
Art Director: Burton Nesbitt Graphic Design
Designers: Amy Milhinch, Chris Bowden,
   Roger Nesbitt

OMEGA TECHNOLOGY IDENTITY

Task

Design an identity for a firm specializing in computer software products and industry consultancy services.

Design Strategies

The initial brief called for an image depicting computer software concepts. The first logo used the five letters in "omega" and created a composition of high-tech "circuitry." Although well received, this concept led to the client changing the brief and requesting a more straightforward, simple approach in impression and presentation. The accepted solution used the omega symbol as a central theme and used bold marks that would maintain their strength when reduced in size.

Design Firm: Burton Nesbitt Graphic Design
Client: Omega Technologies Pty Ltd
Art Director: Burton Nesbitt Graphic Design
Designers: Chris Bowden, Roger Nesbitt,
     Amy Milhinch, Kelly Burton

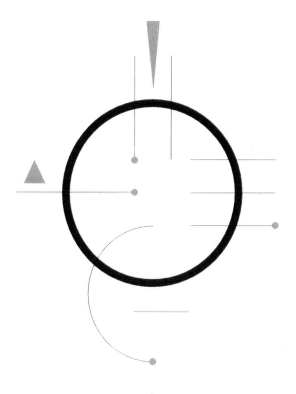

U-17 LOGO

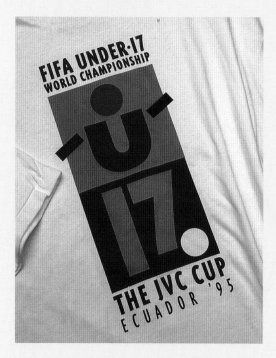

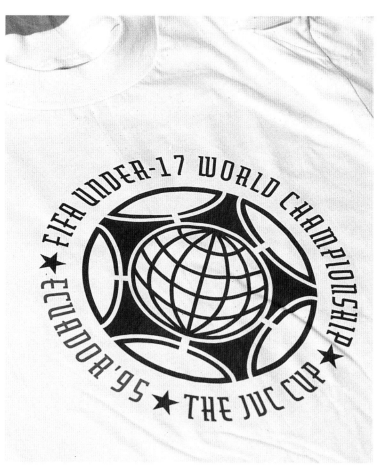

Task

Design an identity for the World Cup soccer series for young people age 17 and under.

Design Strategies

The U-17 soccer series receives worldwide recognition, so all proposed designs had to address several objectives: they had to be international in appearance and color, without emphasizing any particular country or continent; they could not favor either gender, as the games are targeted to both girls and boys; they must look youthful without appearing childish; and they had to easily adapt to animation. The chosen solution incorporated these elements, and added a fresh appeal as well in its graphic approach.

Design Firm: Supon Design Group
Client: ISL Marketing
Art Directors: Supon Phornirunlit,
   Andrew Dolan
Designers: Michael LaManna, Maria Sese
   Paul, John Evans, Rodney Davidson

TRUMPET CLUB BOOK PLATE

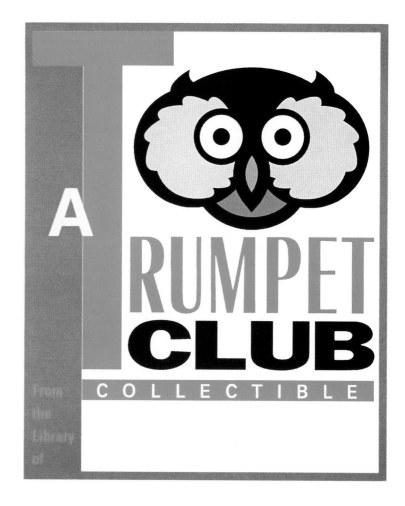

Task

Create a book plate for a publisher's children's book club.

Design Strategies

The client asked for a classic look—not cute or fun, but appealing to boys and girls age 7 to 12. The designers were also restricted in their use of flowers, figures, or animals. Each proposed solution established an identity for the Trumpet book club, and involved the children by providing a space for their names. The chosen piece seemed to create a "shrine" for books, although some of the rejected pieces seemed somewhat more appropriate for the target age group.

Design Firm: Toni Schowalter Design
Client: Bantam Books
Art Director: Toni Schowalter
Designers: Toni Schowalter, Ilene Price

a TRUMPET CLUB COLLECTIBLE

From the Library of

A TRUMPET CLUB COLLECTIBLE

··· From the Library of ···

A TRUMPET CLUB COLLECTIBLE

From the Library of

A TRUMPET CLUB collectible

From the library of

ēSHOP LOGO

ēShop

Task

Design a logo for a firm that creates electronic shopping environments servicing retailers and merchants.

Design Strategies

This design focused on the buying and selling of goods via various components, such as televisions or computers. The client chose the version featuring the spiral "e," which connotes a channel between the consumer and merchant, and communicates the more lively and fun feeling associated with shopping. Enclosing it in a box relates the mark to shopping through a TV or computer.

Design Firm: Mortensen Design
Client: ēShop
Art Director and Designer:
   Gordon Mortensen

ēShop

BROADMOOR BAKER ROLLS PACKAGING

Task

Design packaging that communicates the product's healthful qualities and that stands out among the competitors in a market already saturated with bread products.

Design Strategies

The initial packaging consisted of a six-sided tray with the traditional plastic sack. The package was redesigned, however, to allow easier loading, as well as to help retain the shape of the rolls and protect them from being crushed. The new four-sided package also allowed for easier display on retail shelves.

Design Firm: Hornall Anderson Design
    Works, Inc.
Client: Broadmoor Baker
Art Director: Jack Anderson
Designers: Jack Anderson, Mary Hermes
Illustrator: Scott McDougall

BLOWN AWAY PRINT AND AUDIO/VISUAL ADVERTISING

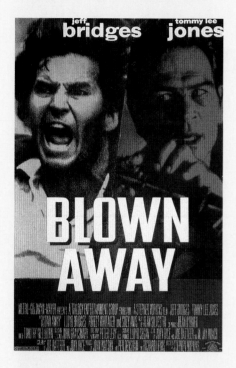

Task

Create advertising that sells an action movie without being exploitative.

Design Strategies

These layouts, all rejected, used conventional action movie concepts supplemented with better designs than those usually found in this genre, so as to indicate the higher quality production of this movie. Graphic looks and photo conversion techniques were packaged with "hip," modern typography. Due to the extraordinary expense of advertising, the executives were unwilling to chance the design improvements and instead chose another title style that had worked successfully for another film.

Design Firm: Mike Salisbury
   Communications, Inc.
Client: MGM
Art Directors: Mike Salisbury, Terry Lamb,
   Scott Binkley
Designers: Mike Salisbury, Terry Lamb

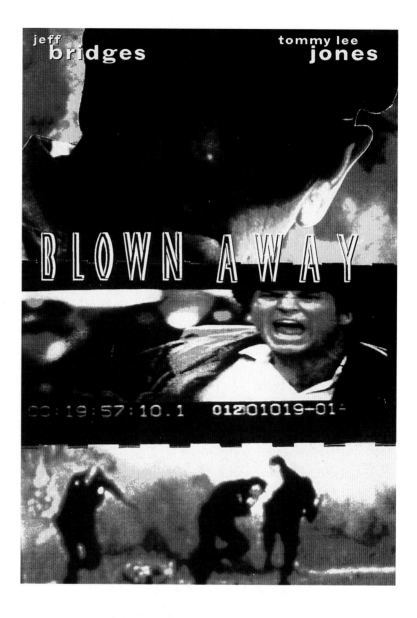

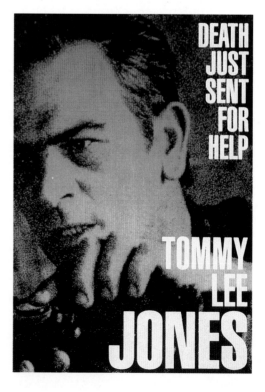

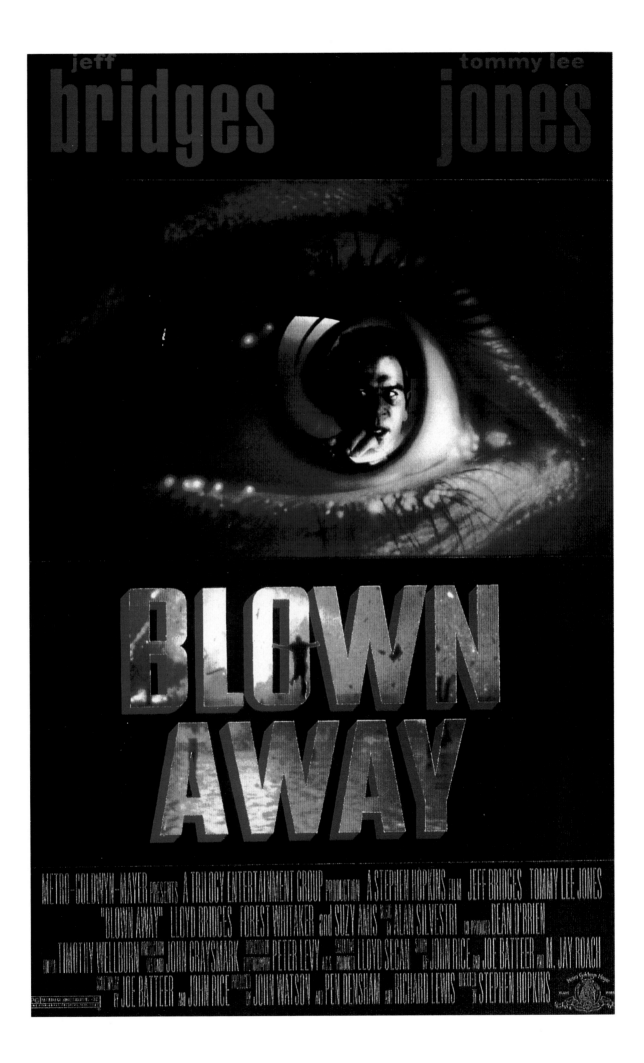

IMAGINARIUM KANGAROOHOP! PACKAGE

Task
Create a package for a children's toy ball.

Design Strategies
The submitted designs all convey a sense of fun and playfulness by showing the toy ball in use, but the selected design incorporated the ball into the logotype itself. The starburst reflects the concept of energy, and multi-colored box panels communicate the idea of fun, while allowing for a multitude of display possibilities. This design also incorporates design elements which will create a family look for a line of products.

Design Firm: Earl Gee Design
Client: Imaginarium
Art Director, Designer, and Illustrator:
   Earl Gee
Photographer: Sandra Frank

70

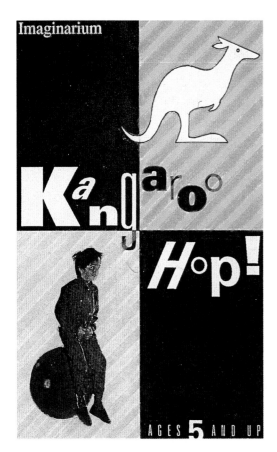

OPERÁRIO BRASIL AWARD SYMBOL

Task
Create a mark for an award honoring Brazilian industry's outstanding response to challenges brought on by new means of production and breakthrough technologies.

Design Strategies
The designers suggested that this annual award portray the creativity and innovation of Brazil's workforce in response to these challenges. One design, ultimately rejected, combined a mechanic's wrench with a lightbulb. The selected logo was deemed a better synthesis of the concept—it portrayed work gloves, machine wheels, and, in the center, a reference to the Brazilian flag.

Design Firm: Interface Designers Ltda
Client: O Globo Newspaper
Art Director: Sérgio Liuzzi
Designer: Gustavo Portela
Illustrators: Sérgio Liuzzi, Gustavo Portela

GULDEN'S TO-GO PACKAGING

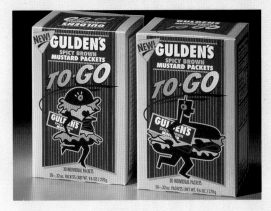

Task

Design the packaging for a box containing individual packets of Gulden's mustard.

Design Strategies

Containers of individual packets of mustard had generally only been marketed to commercial markets. With the introduction of this new product, Gulden's wanted to attract active individuals, consumers who are constantly "on the go." Each of the proposed designs contains the familiar mustard-yellow and red color combination, but combined with updated graphics to suggest movement, speed, and recreation. The selected designs were perhaps the most playful of all—human/sandwich figures carrying their own individual packets of Gulden's mustard.

Design Firm: Wallace Church Associates
Client: American Home Products
Art Director: Stan Church
Designer: Wendy Church
Illustrator: Teri Klass

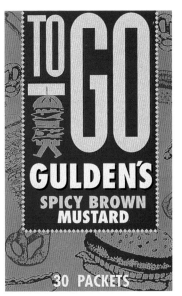

S.W.A.K. (SOME WILD AMERICAN KIDS) PRODUCTS

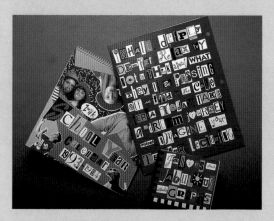

Task

Create a contemporary look to be applied to a line of products targeting girls 8 to 15 years old.

Design Strategies

The designers created 50 distinct looks for consumer test marketing. Of these, a ransom note concept tested highest. The client was also pleased with that solution, but seemed partial to some of the photographic ideas presented. One of the final designs—a combination of both typographic and photographic approaches—was selected as a compromise and applied to multiple products and surfaces.

Design Firm: Sackett Design Associates
Client: Hallmark
Art Director: Mark Sackett
Designers and Illustrators: Mark Sackett, Wayne Sakamoto, James Sakamoto

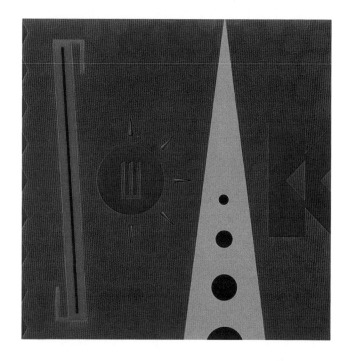

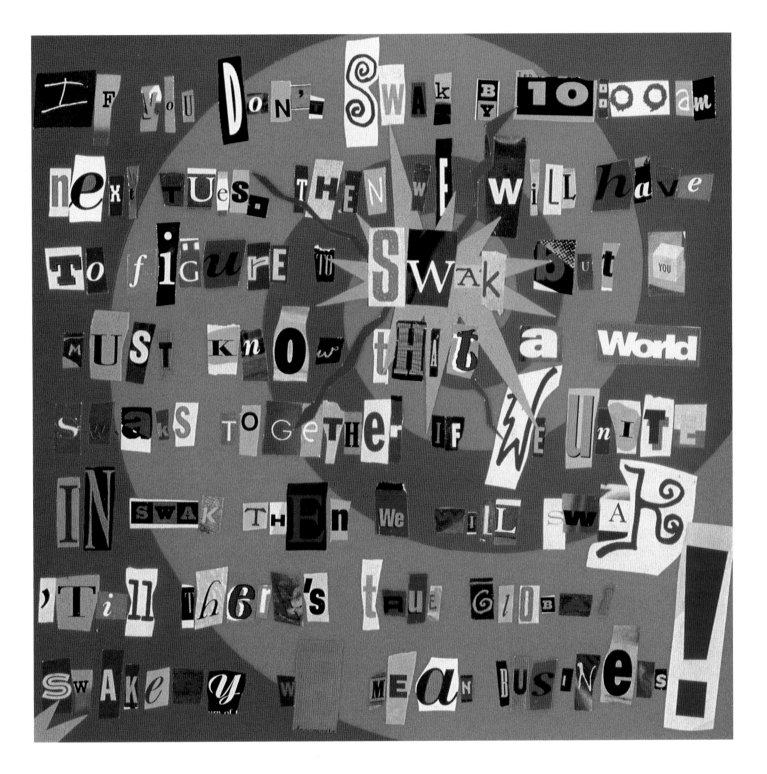

TDK PACKAGING

Task
Update and contemporize the look of audio tape packaging.

Design Strategies
The packaging graphics were used to target the product to specific end-users, denoting music from pop to classical. In some cases, solutions were designed as a series, and graphics indicated lengths of the tape. The accepted design simulated a stack of packaging finishes.

Design Firm: Mike Salisbury
   Communications, Inc.
Client: TDK
Art Director: Mike Salisbury
Designers: Mike Salisbury, Patrick O'Neal
Illustrator: Pat Linse, Terry Lamb

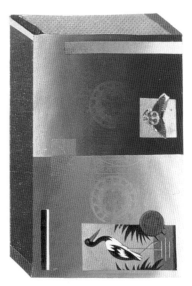

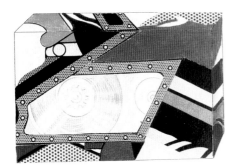

PRODIGY LOGO DESIGN

Task
Redesign a software logo so as to renew its competitive edge.

Design Strategies
All designers interpreted the project so that it appealed to a youthful, "digital" generation of video watchers, a market that consists mainly of young adult males. The chosen design used a lively style that portrayed a sense of movement and dynamics, as well as a clean, uncluttered look that would translate well into a variety of sizes and applications.

Design Firm: Supon Design Group
Client: Prodigy
Art Directors: Supon Phornirunlit, Andrew Dolan
Designers: Maria Sese Paul, Mimi Eanes, Apisak "Eddie" Saibua

K2 SKIS (TRIAXIAL SIDE-CUT)

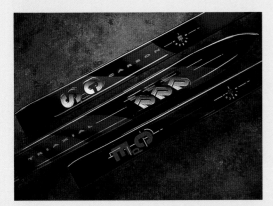

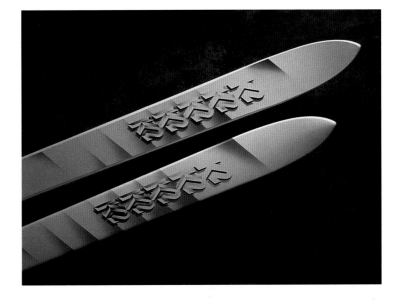

Task

Protect the heritage of the K2 logo chain but incorporate a fashion-inspired ski design.

Design Strategies

The designers recommended a high-tech look for a ski offering fashion, performance, and function. The new Triaxial logo depicts the special construction feature of K2 skis, Triaxial Braiding, which offers the advanced skier excellent response. The primary reason for the client's choosing one ski design over the other was color preference.

Design Firm: Hornall Anderson Design
    Works, Inc.
Client: K2 Corporation
Art Director: Jack Anderson
Designers: Jack Anderson, Mary Hermes,
    John Anicker, Jani Drewfs

SIX SIGMA CAPABILITIES BROCHURE

Task

Promote the blending of Six Sigma with Print NW, a long-established printer.

Design Strategies

Print Northwest's own capabilities brochure, elements of which are shown here, was abandoned because of its merger and name change from Print NW to Print NW/Six Sigma. The first spread of the combined brochure incorporates each company's logo with supportive copy emphasizing themes of consistency and certainty. Capabilities of each of the companies are then highlighted on their own spreads and, once introduced, the motto "The Art of Certainty" is repeated on each spread. The complex, twelve-color brochure itself demonstrates the new entity's capabilities and quality.

Design Firm: Hornall Anderson Design
    Works, Inc.
Client: Print NW/Six Sigma
Art Director: Jack Anderson
Designers: Jack Anderson, Heidi Favour,
    Bruce Branson-Meyer
Photographer: Tom Collicott

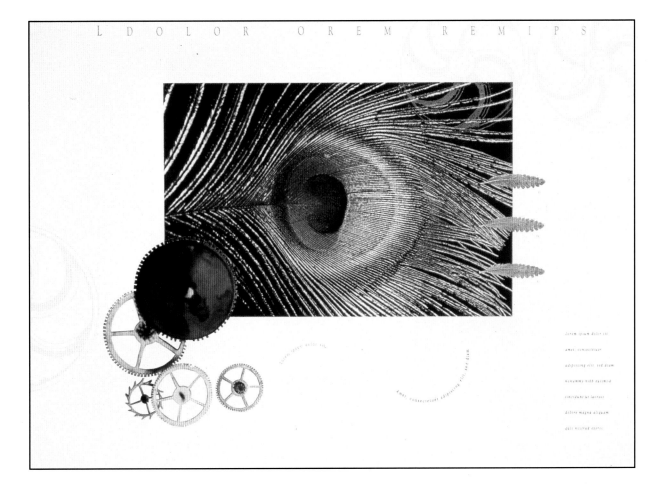

SAFEWAY TOWNHOUSE SALSA AND TACO PACKAGING

Task

Incorporate existing photography and jar configuration into a packaging redesign for this line of Tex-Mex foods.

Design Strategies

Designs for the salsa jar label and taco shell box needed to complement each other. All proposed options were variations on a single theme—illustrative graphics suggestive of native Mexican art combined with existing photos of tomatoes, onions, garlic, and peppers. The final solutions were seemingly chosen based on individual style and design preferences.

Design Firm: Profile Design
Client: Safeway Stores
Art Director: Thomas McNulty
Designers: Brian Jacobson, Anthony Luk

VERTICAL
RECORDS LOGO

VERTICAL

Task

Design a company logo that depicts, without sentimentality, the "divine" nature of a recording label that showcases Christian musicians.

Design Strategies

Rejected designs emphasized images of the extended wings of an angel; a more complete angel form with wings, head, and halo; and a gothic-looking type treatment. The client chose a logo whose type treatment was a more refined gothic. The design eliminated the horizontal strokes on the "E" and "A" to customize and contemporize the treatment. A horizontal oval completes the letter forms and can be interpeted as a halo, or as a compact disc form.

Design Firm: Joseph Rattan Design
Client: Vertical Records
Art Director: Joseph Rattan
Designers: Greg Morgan, Joseph Rattan

VERTICAL

BUCUTI LOGO
AND BROCHURE

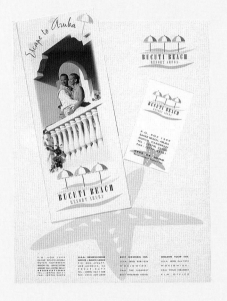

Task
Design a company logo that symbolizes the tropical nature of a Caribbean ocean-side resort.

Design Strategies
To convey the fun and leisure aspects of the resort, the client chose a logo with the threefold aspect of sea, sun, and sand, which also suggested a peaceful holiday through its symmetrical construction and pastel color scheme. Rejected options integrated the client name in "waves" to suggest movement (i.e., a company on the move); as well as a more stylized, modernistic version—the designer's preference—that integrated strong type and graphics.

Design Firm: Graffiti Parc Design
Client: Bucuti Beach Resort Aruba
Art Director and Designer: Laurence Parc

AXENT TECHNOLOGIES, INC. IDENTITY

Task

Design a corporate identity for a computer firm specializing in systems management software.

Design Strategies

The client emphasized that Axent Technologies, Inc. should be portrayed as a strong player in a highly competitive field. After presenting dozens of logo options, an identifying symbol separate from the Axent name was the client's clear preference. The swash forming the cross-bar of the letter "A" of the selected logo portrays the contemporary flair for which the organization is known.

Design Firm: Supon Design Group
Client: Creative Strategy, Inc. for Axent Technologies, Inc.
Art Director and Designer: Andrew Dolan

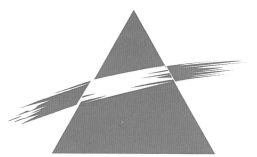

AXENT

AXENT

AXENT

AXENT

AXENT

TOP-FLITE
BRAND IDENTITY

Task

Redesign the packaging for a full line of golf balls, differentiating between the brand's multiple products.

Design Strategies

The market's perception of the Top-Flite brand had fallen below that of its major competitor. One challenge was to simplify the distinctions between product offerings—premium, value-added, and base sub-brands; each available in different trajectory patterns and ball-count sizes. Numerous product logos and packaging options were presented, all of which attempted to better differentiate between products and appeal to the performance-driven consumer. The selected design was very upscale, black and gold solids with a line drawing of the Earth to suggest the brand's worldwide reach.

Design Firm: Wallace Church Associates
Client: Spalding Sports Worldwide
Art Director: Stan Church
Designer: John Waski
Logo Designer: David Ceradini

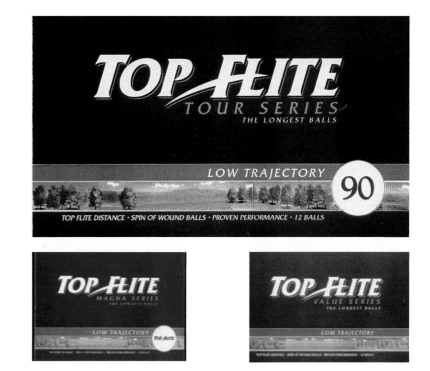

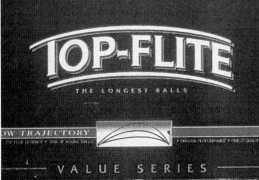

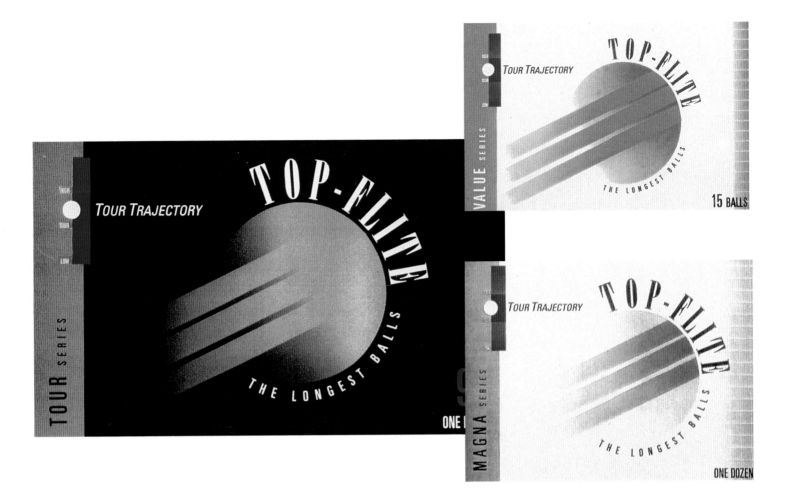

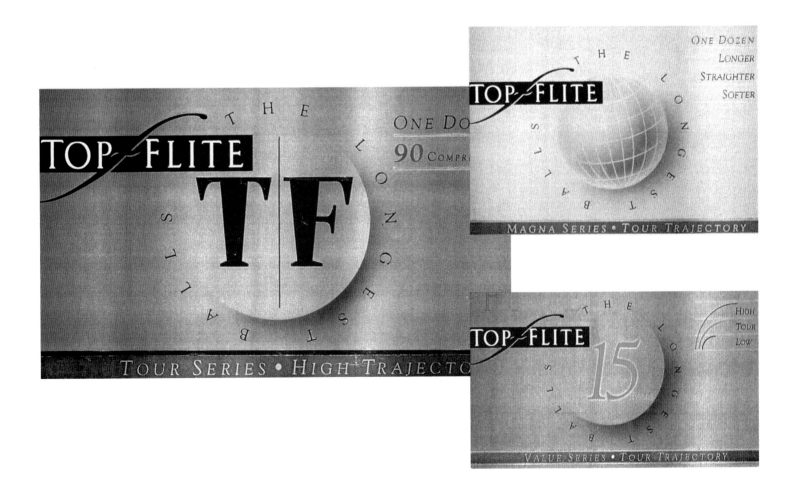

PILLSBURY'S BEST FLOUR IDENTITY

Task

Redesign this brand's imagery to recapture its 100-year heritage of quality.

Design Strategies

As the company's flagship product and oldest brand, Pillsbury's Best Flour plays a critical role in defining the wide range of products under the Pillsbury name. The challenge was to underscore this perception of long-standing quality but also to communicate the brand's compatibility with today's lifestyles. The designers proposed a ribbon motif spanning the Pillsbury logo to represent the flour's excellence. The rejected comp superimposed this graphic onto an engraved-look harvest illustration; the selected design was deemed "cleaner," as it maintained a crisp white background.

Design Firm: Wallace Church Associates
Client: The Pillsbury Company
Art Director: Stan Church
Designer: Joe Cuticone

TOMÉ SOFT
DRINK IDENTITY

Task

Create a brand identity to appeal to
California's huge Hispanic market.

Design Strategies

Derived from the Spanish word meaning
"to drink," the "Tomé" name was to be
combined with icons in a style of art familiar to Latin Americans. Of the many possibilities, one—a graphic portrayal of a pre-
Columbian native and the Mayan pyramid
of Chichen Itza—was rejected as being
"overwhelming." The final choices were
more subtle, primarily combining zigzags
and other random graphics with others
suggestive of nature.

Design Firm: Profile Design
Client: Glencourt Corporation
Art Director: Thomas McNulty
Designer and Illustrator: Brian Jacobson

VAMP PROMOTIONAL MATERIALS

Task

Create a promotion to sell a campy vampire movie featuring an avant-garde rock and roll star.

Design Strategies

A range of looks from total exploitation to "very hip" were developed to capture the mood of the film. The provocative nature was apparent in elements such as lipstick, red lips, and the ever-present fangs. The designer's favorites were the "less is more" editions. The rough illustration is shown here, which was later turned into the completed design and used for the movie.

Design Firm: Mike Salisbury
    Communications, Inc.
Client: 20th Century Fox
Art Director and Designer: Mike Salisbury
Illustrators: Pam Hamilton, Terry Lamb

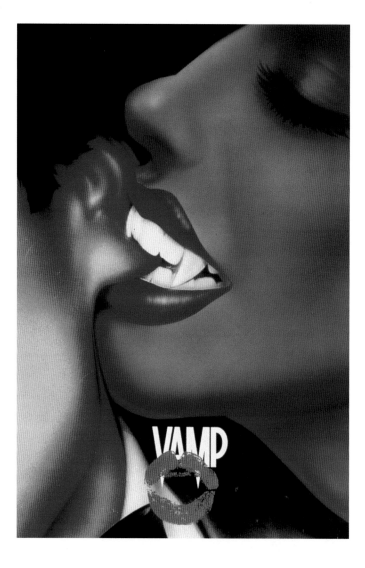

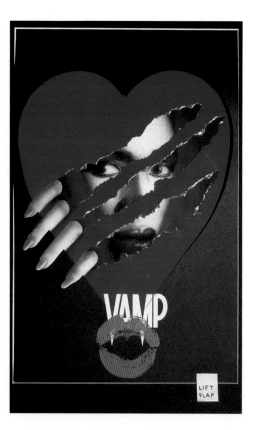

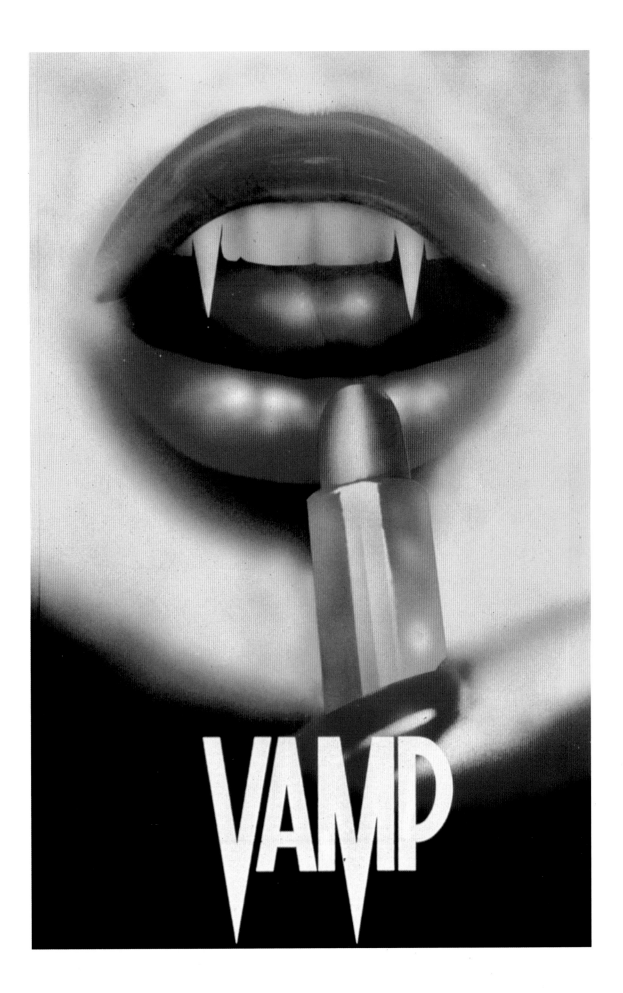

GOOD NATURED CAFE IDENTITY

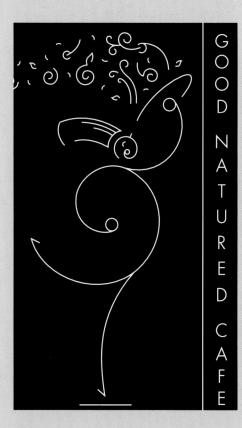

Task
Name and design an identity for an institutional caterer's line of low-fat entrées.

Design Strategies
The designers presented identities for two different proposed names. The designs for Good Natured Cafe emphasized the concept of "light foods" and those for Natural Factory played off the apparent contradiction in the name. Ultimately, the client chose the former for its name and selected the logo because it believed that its airy illustration would more effectively convey the lightness of its product.

Design Firm: SullivanPerkins
Client: Daka International
Art Directors: Andrea Peterson,
   Rob Wilson, Ron Sullivan
Designers: Andrea Peterson,
   Lorraine Charman, Kelly Allen
Copywriters: Christine Lowrance,
   Art Garcia

98

THE NATURAL FACTORY

GOOD NATURED CAFE

good natured cafe

K2 SKIS (8.3 EXTREME)

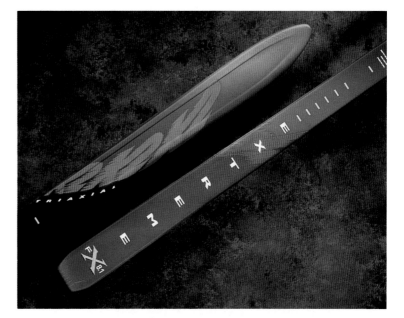

Task

Appeal to young, aggressive skiers with a fashion-inspired ski design.

Design Strategies

The client charged the designers to communicate K2's new, contemporary focus on fashion and balance it with performance and function. A primary consideration was to enhance K2's familiar logo chain design. After seeing the first version, the client decided it wanted a more recreational look for the ski. The new version was preferred for its bolder colors and added sculpture over the flatter ski. Also, the K2 logo chain was embossed on the chosen ski design.

Design Firm: Hornall Anderson Design
    Works, Inc.
Client: K2 Corporation
Art Director: Jack Anderson
Designers: Jack Anderson, David Bates,
    Jani Drewfs

SANYO DEPARTMENT STORE IDENTITY AND PACKAGING

Task
Create an identity that would reposition Sanyo as Japan's "Department Store of the Future."

Design Strategies
The designers presented dozens of logo and packaging options, each portraying slightly different takes on Sanyo's desire to be seen as a modern, but neighborly, all-inclusive retailer. Finalists included a shining star graphic, portraying Sanyo's distinctiveness; a bold, architectural mix of squares and an "S," depicting progressiveness with a personal touch; and the final choice—an elegant arc over the Sanyo name. This symbol suggests the sun, the Earth's life source.

Design Firm: Profile Design
Client: Sanyo Department Store (Japan)
Art Director: Kenichi Nishiwaki
Designer: Profile Design

BROADMOOR BAKER BREAD PACKAGING

Task

Design packaging that would have a shelf impact, communicate the product's qualities and health benefits, and encourage future purchases.

Design Strategies

The initial design featured a box-like package, and was rejected because of the lack of visual display needed to enhance the product. The box was replaced by a tray within a traditional, protective plastic sack to help retain the bread's shape. The resulting solution conveys the product's high-quality, natural ingredients, which are emphasized with a large type treatment. It establishes its upscale position, and uses "baker's white" colors rather than the Earth tones typical of the competitors' products.

Design Firm: Hornall Anderson Design
    Works, Inc.
Client: Broadmoor Baker
Art Director: Jack Anderson
Designers: Jack Anderson, Jani Drewfs,
    Mary Hermes
Illustrator: Scott McDougall

PENSOFT PERSPECTIVE SOFTWARE PACKAGING

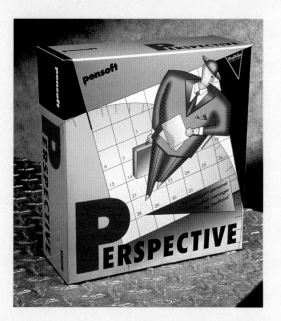

Task

Design a packaging program for a personal information management software for users of pen-based computers.

Design Strategies

All designs, both rejected and accepted, needed strong shelf appeal, as well as the ability to reproduce effectively in small sizes for mail order catalogs. The selected design emphasized the concept of putting your time, schedule, and meetings into "perspective," symbolized by a businessman walking over a clock arc and calendar grid while checking his watch.

Design Firm: Earl Gee Design
Client: Pensoft Corporation
Art Directors: Earl Gee, Fani Chung
Designers: Earl Gee, Fani Chung
Illustrators: Earl Gee, David Bottoms

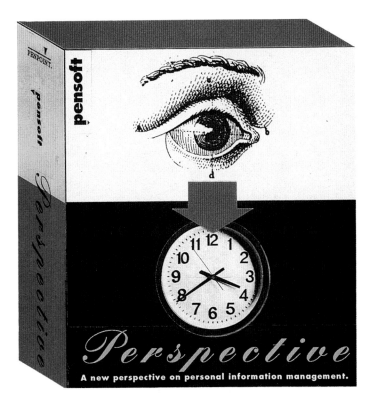

GREAT REJECTS

What's the difference between rejects and truly great rejects? You'll see for yourself in this section.

These rejected solutions were proposed in presentations, but never made the final cut. Although they're all outstanding works, there are any number of reasons why they were ultimately rejected: perhaps they didn't quite match the client's vision, or a targeted focus group didn't choose them. Possibly, the business which contracted the studio failed before the design was produced. The project may have gone to someone else for internal reasons that were purely political. In a few cases, the design was accepted, but the client did not pay the studio, so the final art was not delivered. There may not be a single strategy to determine why clients choose what they do, but good design is good design, regardless of whether it was ever published, and here you'll see some of the best.

S-DESIGNOR
ADVERTISEMENT

Task
Redesign existing advertising to emphasize product name, theme, and call for action.

Design Strategies
Fire was added to the pepper design to enliven it and better symbolize the "hot" theme. Typography was rearranged in a clearer, more hierarchical format, and the originality and innovation of the product was emphasized. The solution, however, was rejected in favor of a less expensive, internal resource.

Design Firm: Laughing Dog Creative, Inc.
Client: SDP Technologies
Art Director and Designer: Frank EE Grubich
Illustrator: Tony Klausen

THE AVENUE IDENTITY

Task

Create an identity for a new residential housing development.

Design Strategies

With a vast number of rose bushes featured throughout the development, the client wanted to incorporate a floral emblem as part of the design. The development itself would provide an interesting mix of upscale, medium-density housing. The "name plate" identity worked well, and the floral emblem could also be used as a separate entity on mailboxes, front doors, keyrings, etc. The design was ultimately rejected, however, when the client decided to produce an alternative design in-house.

Design Firm: Burton Nesbitt Graphic Design
Client: Delfin Property Group
Art Director: Burton Nesbitt Graphic Design
Designers: Kelly Burton, Roger Nesbitt

CHILDREN'S BATH PRODUCTS

Task

Design silkscreened labels for a line of children's and infants' bath products for distribution to high-end stores and boutiques.

Design Strategies

The design firm's research showed most upscale bath products featured simple, minimally designed labels with the look of old-fashioned apothecary goods. Using that vision as their guidepost, they added a sense of childlike whimsy. A favorite design combined the labeled look with a secondary screen around the package so that, even empty, the bottle was still appealing. The project, however, was never produced.

Design Firm: The Q Design Group, Ltd.
Client: Nature's Bubbles
Art Director, Designer and Illustrator:
    Christine DiGuiseppi

TWO-CAN LOGO

Task

Design a corporate identity for a children's book publisher that encourages adult-child participation in reading.

Design Strategies

A simple twist creates a "2" out of a toucan, which was designed to appear friendly to children and to make a strong company endorsement to adults. The publisher's invoice was even renamed "Bill," with the toucan's bill tinted for greater effect. Unfortunately, the company never got off the ground, so the design was not produced.

Design Firm: Minale, Pattersfield + Partners Ltd
Client: Two-Can Publishers
Art Director and Designer: Steve Dowson

TWO·CAN
EDUCATIONAL BOOKS FOR CHILDREN

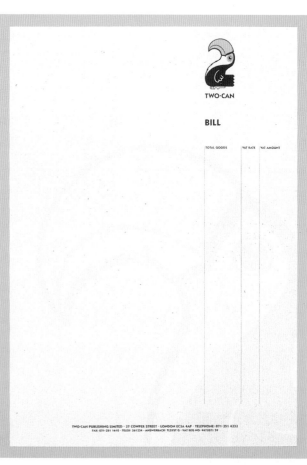

DINAH SHORE'S SOUP PACKAGING

Task
Design a package that successfully markets home-style soups from Dinah Shore's recipes.

Design Strategies
Three different package configurations were explored for the product's design: a square box, canister, and bag. Various graphic styles included product depiction through photos, as well as illustrations of Dinah Shore. The packaging was meant to project a home-style soup made with natural ingredients that is more convenient for today's lifestyle and busy schedule. The product, however, never made it past the comp stage because the client decided not to pursue the project.

Design Firm: Hornall Anderson Design
    Works, Inc.
Client: Dinah Shore
Art Director and Designer: Julia LaPine

FLYING ACES IDENTITY & PACKAGING

Task

Create an identity and packaging design for a new toy called Flying Aces with a shelf presence that would appeal to children.

Design Strategies

A series of logo studies were done that would appropriately reflect the "Flying Aces" image for the toy market. Logos, which first went through black and white studies, used enhanced red, white, and blue colors to give them a patriotic feel. The comp packaging designs included both illustration and photography styles. The project, however, was discontinued before any designs were produced.

Design Firm: Hornall Anderson Design Works, Inc.
Client: Hasbro Toys/Flying Aces
Art Director: Jack Anderson
Designers: Jack Anderson, David Bates, Jani Drewfs

FLYING ACES IDENTITY & PACKAGING

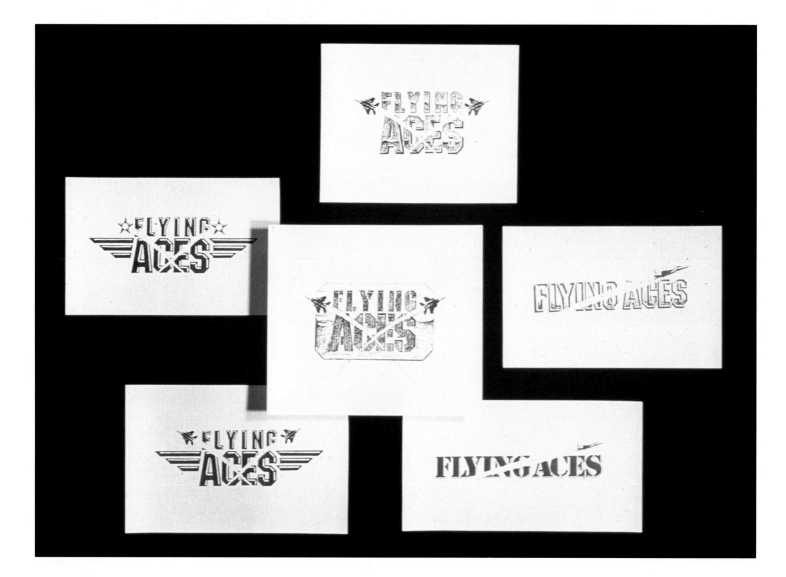

ELITE
WARRIORS
OF THE
SKY!

Lorum ips
gkfdzy asom
frouer rselt
sequen

um ipsom
gkfdzy as
frouer rselt
sequen

PLANETE DETERGENT AND PLANETE COOKIES

Task

Design a name, logo, and packaging applications for a brand of grocery products.

Design Strategies

The designs that were submitted were conceived to promote a unique personality while telling a specific product benefit story about taste (cookies) or effectiveness (detergent). The chosen strategy focused on a natural, honest approach that delivered two messages: that the products were of high quality, and that health and environmental consciousness need not be at the expense of fun.

Design Firm: TAXI Design
Client: Oshawa Foods
Art Director, Designer, and Illustrator:
    Jane Hope

PUBLIC WORKS
CANADA LOGO

Task

Design a new corporate mark for the department of public works.

Design Strategies

The intent of this design was to present the client as management specialists who employ the most up-to-date technology available. The mark, based on the image of a computer chip, incorporates symbols relating to architecture—such as bridges, canals, public buildings, and their associated services. Although this design was initially accepted, another mark that was later created internally ultimately became the chosen solution due to political reasons at the client's office.

Design Firm: Neville Smith Graphic Design
Client: Public Works Canada
Art Director, Designer, and Illustrator:
    Neville Smith

AHATA LOGO

Task

Design a company logo that preserves the corporate aspect of an association representing the Aruba hotel and business community, and also depicts its tropical identity.

Design Strategies

One proposed solution emphasized the ampersand in the client's name to introduce a looser design element and integrate sun rays, indicating the Caribbean location. Other versions incorporated design elements illustrating sea, sky, and sun, and used illustrative island graphics as a backdrop for typography, while focusing on the acronym AHATA. The project, however, was put on indefinite hold.

Design Firm: Graffiti Parc Design
Client: Aruba Hotel and Tourism
   Association
Art Director: Laurence Parc
Designers: Zindine Aksa, Laurence Parc

120

121

AMS LOGO

Task

Create a logo for a branch of an airline to show the technical aspect of the service while preserving its human dimension.

Design Strategies

One logo suggested a compass's precision, used with a cartoon-like airplane to keep it informal. Planes in flight were employed to suggest skill and the importance of improved technology. Emphasizing the AMS acronym provided effective recognition for the client. Colors used are less institutional to personalize the logos. The project, however, was later put on hold by the client.

Design Firm: Graffiti Parc Design
Client: Air Canada
Art Director and Designer: Zindine Aksa

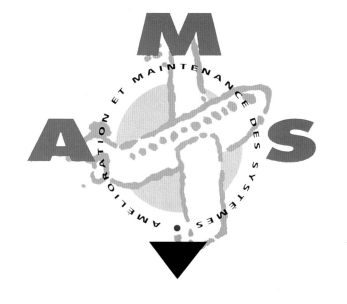

THE WARNER BROS. TELEVISION LOGO

Task
Design a logo for a new television network with programming directed to young people.

Design Strategies
To identify their new television network, the client wanted a distinctive look, but one that was readily linked with its famous Warner Bros. shield. In addition, the identity needed to attract a young audience with its vitality, while maintaining simplicity. The designers submitted both stylized, modern versions and conservative ones that adhered closely to the traditional Warner Bros. image. Unfortunately, these solutions, although well received by the client, were not chosen for the project.

Design Firm: Supon Design Group
Client: The Warner Bros. Television
Art Directors: Supon Phornirunlit,
   Andrew Dolan
Designer: Apisak "Eddie" Saibua

BRIO
TRAIN PARTY
PRODUCT LINE

Task

Design an entirely new line of party goods whose design was integrated with the existing toy line.

Design Strategies

The designers created the actual products, packaging, and point-of-sale display graphics, as well as the names for both the "Brio Train Party Kit" product line and the "Party Depot" display. The bright colors were derived from the palette of the toys themselves. The clean, understated, yet bold approach complemented the toys. The client, however, contracted another design firm closer to their offices to complete the project.

Design Firm: THARP DID IT
Client: BRIO Toys of Sweden
Art Director: Rick Tharp
Designers: Amy Bednarek, Jana Heer,
    Debra Naeve, Laurie Okamura,
    Rick Tharp
Product Development: Jane Krejci

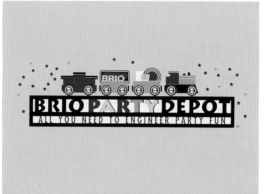

INDUSTRIAL ARTS INFORMATION POSTER

Task

Design an informational poster for a branch of government.

Design Strategies

The traditional industrial arts are recognized by a seal called "Rogo Mark," which indicates the qualified approval of the Kyoto Prefectural Government. The poster conveyed a conservative yet intriguing dimension to this government division. The client later decided to use another Rogo Mark that displayed a Japanese character called "kyo," however, and rejected this design. Shortly thereafter, the project was put on indefinite hold.

Design Firm: Shima Design Office Inc.
Client: Kyoto Prefectural Government
Art Director, Designer, and Illustrator:
  Takahiro Shima

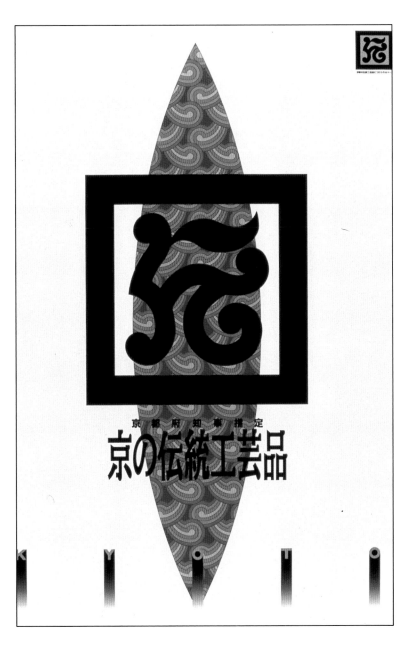

UNITED WAY POSTER

Task

Design a poster that would have an immediate impact, break away from photographic stereotypes of past campaigns, and be used regionally with the potential for national distribution.

Design Strategies

The tumbling graphic elements imply an unstable situation associated with institutions, groups, or individuals in need of assistance. At the bottom of the visual is a safety net positioned to catch or assist those in need. Following a visual presentation and much debate, a political decision was made to return to the more familiar images of people used in previous campaigns.

Design Firm: Neville Smith Graphic Design
Client: The United Way
Art Director, Designer, and Illustrator: Neville Smith

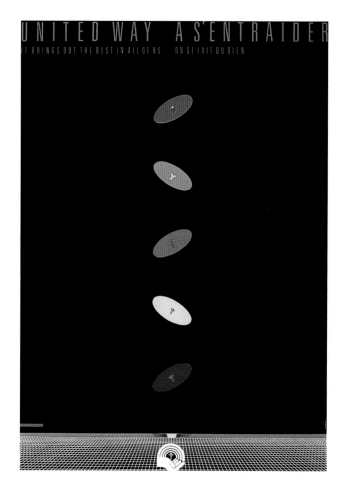

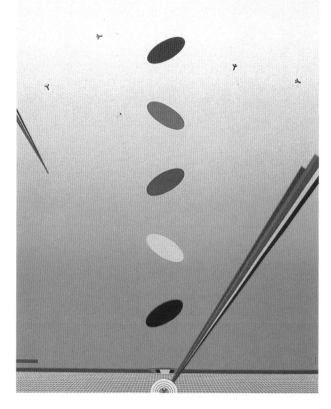

126

HAMBERDOG
IDENTITY

Task
Design an identity for a hot dog–shaped hamburger product.

Design Strategies
The designers created these cheerful canine characters to communicate the hybrid nature of the product—a hamburger that looks like a hot dog. The informality of the food was also illustrated. The client liked the visuals, but the funding for the project fell through and the effort was suspended.

Design Firm: SullivanPerkins
Client: Heartland
Art Director: Ron Sullivan
Designer: Rob Wilson

MELTON WAVES IDENTITY

Task

Design a corporate identity program for a suburban leisure center.

Design Strategies

Both versions, which were ultimately rejected, created symbols that could be applied to signage at the complex, while it captured the relaxed feel of the pool/leisure center. The initials "MW" of Melton Waves lent themselves to an interesting image as if reflected in a pool of water. An alternative option illustrated activities that can be found at the leisure center. The concept also allowed for the individual components of the complete design to be used on signage.

Design Firm: Cozzolino Ellett Design D'Vision Pty. Ltd.
Client: Melton Waves Leisure Centre
Art Director: Mimmo Cozzolino
Designer and Illustrator: Phil Ellett
Computer Operator: Mike McHugh

SHOWERS

MELTON WAVES
LEISURE CENTRE

POOL ATTENDANTS

orem ipsum dolor sit amet, consectetuer adipiscing elit, sed diam nonummy nibh euismod tincidunt ut laoreet dolore magna aliquam erat volutpat. Ut wisi enim ad minim veniam, quis nostrud exerci tation ullamcorper suscipit lobortis nisl ut aliquip ex ea commodo consequat.

Duis autem vel eum iriure dolor in hendrerit in vulputate velit esse molestie consequat, vel illum dolore eu feugiat nulla

SITSDMET, ADIPISCING ELIT HEP DIAM NONUMMY NIB PHONE 123 4567 FAXM DOLOR SIT AMET, SED NIBH CONSECTETUE

POOL ATTENDANTS

Lorem ipsum dolor sit amet, consectetuer adipiscing elit, sed diam nonummy nibh euismod tincidunt ut laoreet dolore magna aliquam erat volutpat. Ut wisi enim ad minim veniam, quis nostrud exerci tation ullamcorper suscipit lobortis nisl ut aliquip ex ea commodo consequat.

Duis autem vel eum iriure dolor in hendrerit in vulputate velit esse molestie consequat, vel illum dolore eu feugiat nulla facilisis at nostrud exerci tation ullamcorper suscipit lobortis nisl ut aliquip ex ea commodo

MELTON WAVES
LEISURE CENTRE

SITSDMET, ADIPISCING ELIT HEP DIAM NONUMMY NIB PHONE 123 4567 FAXM DOLOR SIT AMET, SED NIBH

CAFE

QUINTESSENCE GROUP LOGO

Task
Design a logo for a marketing firm.

Design Strategies
Although its financial backing dwindled before this company could become established, its identity was meant to attract an upscale, corporate clientele. One logo design emphasized the initial "Q," playing off the organization's tagline "The Q Factor." Others were primarily typographic, some with playful graphics added for visual interest.

Design Firm: SullivanPerkins
Client: The Quintessence Group
Art Director: Ron Sullivan
Designer: Rob Wilson

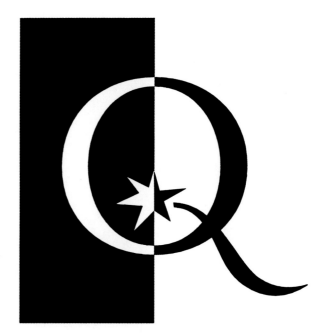

LEVI'S 505 AND 506 LABELING

Task

Design new labeling for Levi Strauss & Co.'s 500 jeans series.

Design Strategies

Levi asked the designers to give a richer, more premium look and feel to its jeans while improving on the label and its ability to communicate the proper fit to the consumer. Market testing favored keeping much of the equity of the existing brand identity, including Levi's stock of illustrations. Both of the presented designs fulfilled this objective, but not to the extent desired by the client. Therefore, both were rejected in favor of those of another firm.

Design Firm: Sackett Design Associates
Client: Levi Strauss & Co.
Art Director: Mark Sackett
Designers: Mark Sackett,
    Wayne Sakamoto

STREETS OF FIRE
PROMOTION

Task

Create a logo that could be used as a poster to promote a fantasy movie with a rock and roll theme whose primary audience is under age 35.

Design Objectives

To depict the action-filled film, the designers used appropriate elements to appeal to its young adult audience (e.g., fire, motorcycle paraphernalia, neon). All were rejected in favor of another design which also conveyed the entertainment value of the film, as well as its "dark" side.

Design Firm: Mike Salisbury
   Communications, Inc.
Client: Universal Pictures
Art Director: Mike Salisbury
Designers: Terry Lamb, Todd Waite,
   Tom Nikosey

UTILICORP NEWSLETTER/ MAGAZINE

Task

Redesign an internal newsletter/magazine which targets the employees of all worldwide divisions of UtiliCorp.

Design Strategies

The objective was to alter the publication from what was typically the more pedestrian format of a newsletter into the more readable and interesting editorial format of a magazine. The client liked the initial spreads shown here and was very enthusiastic about the proposed change. After a thorough assessment of its resources, however, UtiliCorp concluded that it could not accommodate such an ambitious reconfiguration.

Design Firm: Sackett Design Associates
Client: UtiliCorp United Inc.
Art Director: Mark Sackett
Designers and Illustrators: Mark Sackett,
   Wayne Sakamoto, James Sakamoto

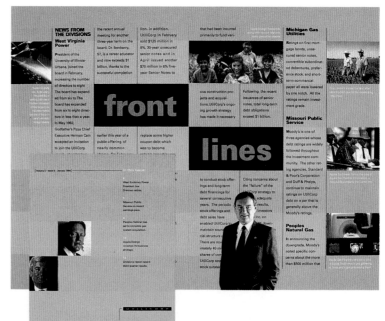

FRETTE LOGO

Task

Design an identity for an Italian manufacturer of household linen for both the traditional "matrimonial" market and a more mass-market printed range.

Design Strategies

In an effort to find a design that would suit both ranges, the proposed solution emphasizes the weave of the material—a fundamental element of the client's business success. The identity also has a traditional, exclusive feel, making it wholly appropriate for the company's target audience. The new range, however, was not produced.

Design Firm: Minale, Pattersfield +
  Partners Ltd
Client: Frette
Art Director: Marcello Minale
Designer: Ian Delaney

SUNRISE FARMS BUTTER TUBS PACKAGING

Task

Create packaging concept ideas for the Washington State Dairy Association's flavored butters.

Design Strategies

Illustrations represented the actual Breakfast Butter flavors, while photographs were used to depict the Dinner Butters. A warmer color palette was chosen for the breakfast flavors, while the dinner flavors had bolder colors. Ultimately, the ideas were well received, but the project never made it past the comp stage.

Design Firm: Hornall Anderson Design
   Works, Inc.
Client: Sunrise Farms
Art Director: John Hornall

MIAMI TO GO
IDENTITY

Task

Design an identity for a line of stores that cater to tourists in Miami.

Design Strategies

Tourists traveling to this exciting resort city are looking for an exotic, fun-filled destination. The designers chose to promote these qualities in their designs for the store's identity: a fanciful flamingo, a frolicking dolphin, a pre-Hispanic glyph, and a day/night graphic of the city. The client was pleased with the presentation, but, unfortunately, Miami To Go never got going.

Design Firm: SullivanPerkins
Client: Miami To Go
Art Director: Ron Sullivan
Designers: Lorraine Charman, Kelly Allen,
    Rob Wilson

RETURN TO THE BLUE LAGOON ADVERTISING

Task

Create a design that would sell the sequel to a successful, romantic location film that also had an element of soft-core sex in it.

Design Objectives

All the solutions submitted attempted to capture a feeling of romance and location with great graphics with hints at South Seas traditions, à la Gauguin. Lush tropical settings, water, and sun surround the film's young characters. Of these numerous ideas, none were accepted for this project, which eventually used another style.

Design Firm: Mike Salisbury
   Communications, Inc.
Client: Tri-Star Pictures
Art Director and Designer: Mike Salisbury
Illustrators: Brian Sisson, Pam Hamilton,
   Pat Linse

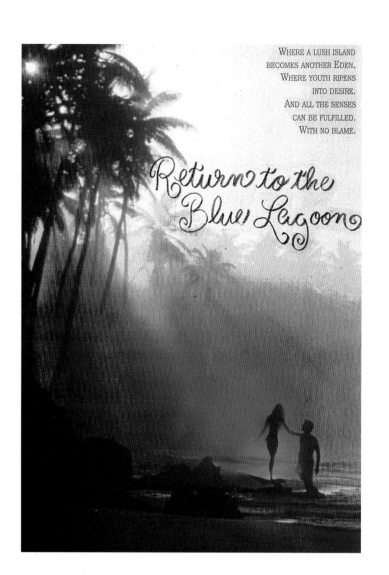

COME BACK
TO THE BLUE LAGOON.
WHERE A LUSH ISLAND
BECOMES ANOTHER EDEN.
WHERE YOUTH RIPENS
INTO DESIRE.
AND ALL THE SENSES
CAN BE FULFILLED.
WITH NO BLAME.

*Return
to the
Blue Lagoon*

TWO CHILDREN
ORPHANS IN A LUSH,
TROPICAL PARADISE,
UNFAMILIAR WITH THEIR SEX
OR THEIR CIVILIZATION.
AWAKEN TO EACH OTHER.
WITH CONFUSION, JOY AND
A NATURAL FULFILLMENT.

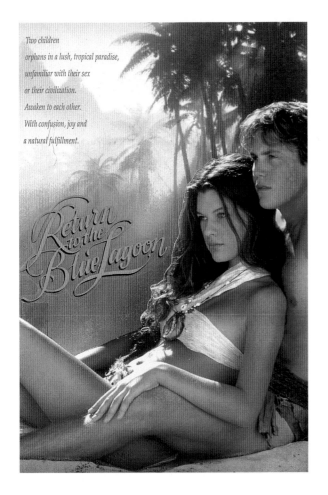

Two children

orphans in a lush, tropical paradise,

unfamiliar with their sex

or their civilization.

Awaken to each other.

With confusion, joy and

a natural fulfillment.

TWO CHILDREN
ORPHANS IN A LUSH, TROPICAL
PARADISE,
UNFAMILIAR WITH THEIR SEX
OR THEIR CIVILIZATION.
AWAKEN TO EACH OTHER.
WITH CONFUSION, JOY AND
A NATURAL FULFILLMENT.

ASYMETRIX POCKETBOOK PACKAGING

Task
Create a family look for this series of program enhancements for the ToolBook brand of software.

Design Strategies
The initial objective was to create these brochures to be merchandised at the cash register like paperback books. The product and its packaging, therefore, would need to be small and convenient, and convey an inexpensive price point. Only one of the first three products (the DayBook) was taken past the comprehensive stage; the rest of the series was not realized.

Design Firm: Hornall Anderson Design Works, Inc.
Client: Asymetrix Corporation
Art Director: Jack Anderson
Designers: Jack Anderson, Julie Lock, Mary Hermes

ASYMETRIX COMPEL PACKAGING

Task

Design packaging for Asymetrix's Compel software product that would make it stand out from its competitors on retail shelves.

Design Strategies

Two different design solutions were presented for Compel's packaging. Both used similar illustrative-style graphics, but with different type treatments for the product logo itself. The designers and client alike thought that these designs were visually more appealing than the typical computer software packaging. At the comp stage, however, the project was put on hold.

Design Firm: Hornall Anderson Design
    Works, Inc.
Client: Asymetrix Corporation
Art Director: Jack Anderson
Designers: Jack Anderson, Julie Lock

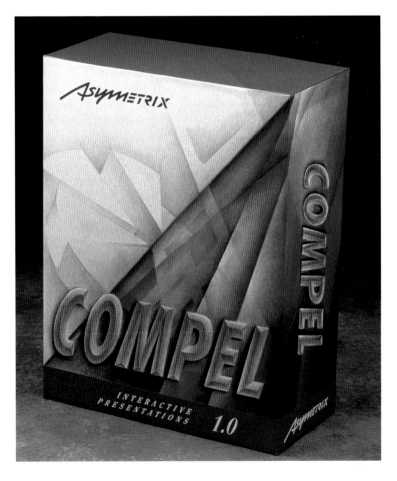

LEGENDS OF THE FALL PRINT ADVERTISING

Task

Develop print advertising to sell a cast of famous stars in a romantic period movie with heavy production value.

Design Strategies

To overcome the disadvantage that period movies traditionally have in the marketplace, the designers developed looks that had a fashion feeling, e.g., posters that look like pages from a magazine. The rejected pieces presented various elements of this concept. The final design used components of these rejected pieces to make a whole.

Design Firm: Mike Salisbury
    Communications, Inc.
Client: Tri-Star Pictures
Art Director: Mike Salisbury
Designers: Mike Salisbury, Scott Binkley,
    Pat Linse, Jack Upston

FRUITFUL PARTNERSHIPS ANNUAL REPORT

Task

Create concept proposals for the client's annual report, based on the "partnership" theme.

Design Strategies

The designers sought an innovative concept reinforced by stimulating visuals that reflect the creative and sometimes unusual solutions the client provides for its customers. The concept, which was rejected, took customer case histories and applied fruit images—red currants, for example—to suggest the client's involvement in the project. The images of the whole pear on the front cover and half pear on the back subtly underscore the partnership theme.

Design Firm: Tor Pettersen & Partners Ltd
Client: Logica
Art Directors: Tor Pettersen, David Brown
Designer: Laura Fortescue
Illustrator: David Hunter

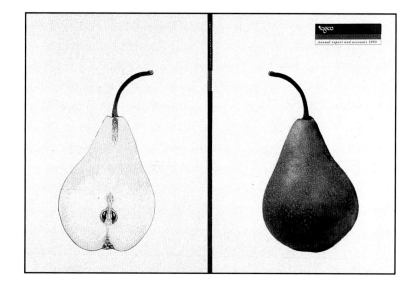

RAPTIS PACIFIC IDENTITY

Task
Redesign an identity for a corporation involved in the gathering and distribution of seafood throughout Pacific Asia.

Design Strategies
This identity needed to reflect the "fresh seas" quality of the product range. Rather than depicting specific items of seafood, the designers opted for a more all-encompassing image that could appear on packaging for a wide range of products, as well as on corporate stationery. The wave element seemed to address these objectives. The client, however, decided to delay the introduction of a new identity.

Design Firm: Burton Nesbitt Graphic Design
Client: Raptis Pacific
Art Director: Burton Nesbitt Graphic Design
Designers: Kelly Burton, Roger Nesbitt

GOTCHA IDENTITY

Task

Create an identity to both recapture a surfwear company's traditional customers and reposition the company towards a broader, older target audience.

Design Strategies

In print pieces, you must choose words carefully, or render them meaningless. Graphics also have drawbacks: they can too easily put products in a niche, or date the look. The designers chose not to use words or graphics, instead imbedding the message in the photography. Though dynamic and sporting plenty of attitude, none of these logos was chosen.

Design Firm: Mike Salisbury
   Communications, Inc.
Client: Gotcha Sportswear
Art Director and Designer: Mike Salisbury
Illustrators: Terry Lamb, Brian Sisson,
   Pat Linse

RADIO PICTURES LOGO

Task

Create a logo for a client's motion picture division that was producing a period movie.

Design Strategies

To convey the 1930s flavor echoed in the film, the designer created a composition that combined the classic RKO studio and RCA logos. Its original inspiration, however, was a decades-old German letterform. This version, which was eventually rejected, was drawn by hand.

Design Firm: Mike Salisbury
   Communications, Inc.
Client: Lucas Film
Art Director and Designer: Mike Salisbury
Illustrator: Jim Wood

BLASTING POWDER PACKAGING

Task

Design packaging for a new confectionary product with a "super hot" cinnamon flavor aimed at the under-12 market.

Design Strategies

With a comic direction in mind, the designers used the window that the client wanted to appear on the box as the character's hair. A comic book letterer was contracted to ensure authenticity of type. The product was shelved, however, after focus groups determined that its powdery form was too troublesome to contain, as well as too suggestive of illegal substances.

Design Firm: Laughing Dog Creative, Inc.
Client: Brach's
Art Director: Frank EE Grubich
Designer: Tim Mikulski
Illustrator: Tim Mikulski
Typographers: Mike Heisler, Tim Mikulski

THE GOLDEN LIGHT ILLUSTRATED BOOK

Task

Create and write an illustrated children's book.

Design Strategies

The book tells the story of catching a fish, from the fish's point of view. The square of color represents the fish's small, safe world, toned with soft blues and greens. The human world is depicted using harsh reds and yellows. Although the book is complete, to date, it has not found a publisher.

Design Firm: Trudy Cole-Zielanski Design
Art Director, Designer, and Illustrator:
Trudy Cole-Zielanski

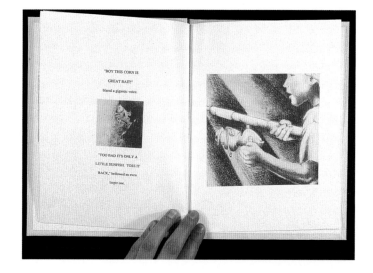

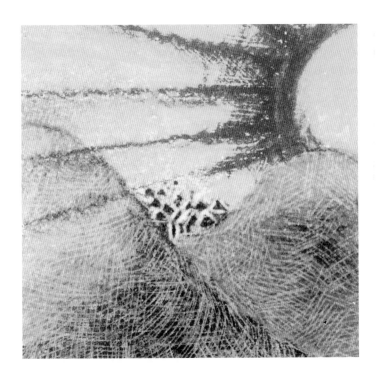 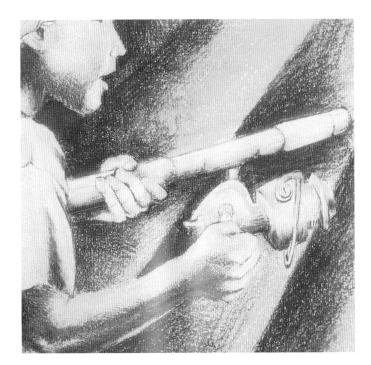

 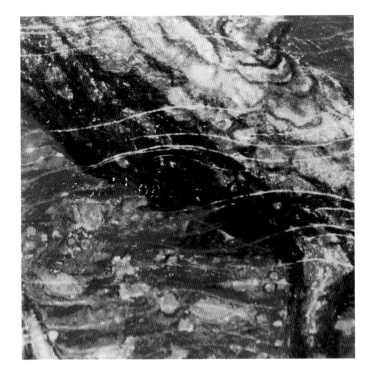

DIADORA SHOE BOX PACKAGING

Task

Design shoe box packaging that provides a stronger image in the client's domestic (Italian) athletic shoe market, and that could also be adjusted for a separate look in the international market.

Design Strategies

Initially, the box consisted solely of one design: a white box with red and green graphics. After exploring several color and design concepts, the final solution became a black lid on white, red, green, or black colored bottoms, depending on the shoe style e.g., tennis, running, etc.). The black-lid boxes became the series seen in the international market, while the original white, red, and green boxes continued to be used in the domestic market. But the basic colors in both markets remained white, green, and red—the colors of Italy—and all packaging included the trademark logo "swish" of Diadora USA.

Design Firm: Hornall Anderson Design
    Works, Inc.
Client: Diadora USA
Art Director: Jack Anderson
Designers: Jack Anderson, David Bates,
    Juliet Shen

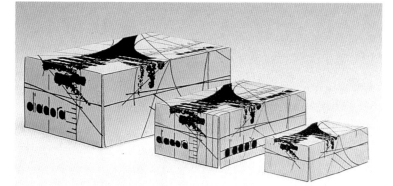

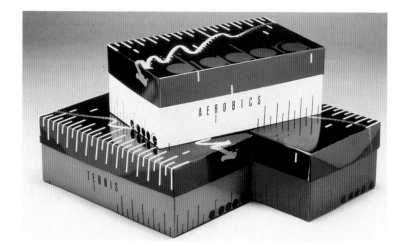

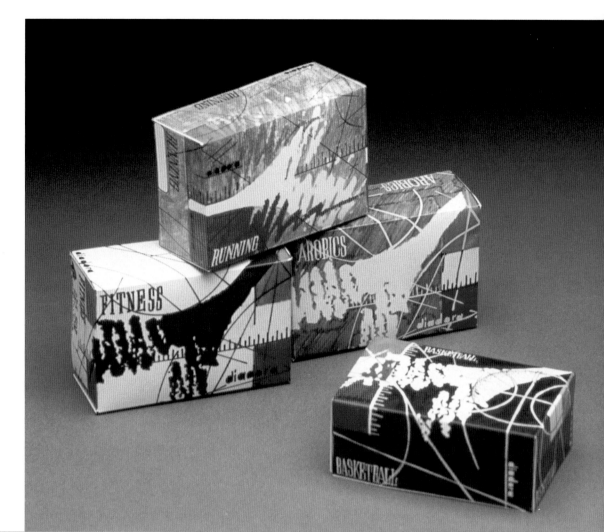

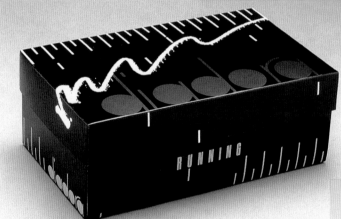

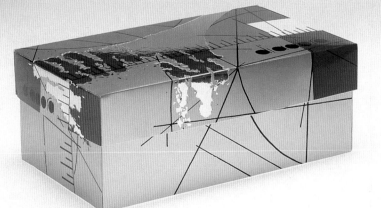

DIADORA SHOE BOX PACKAGING

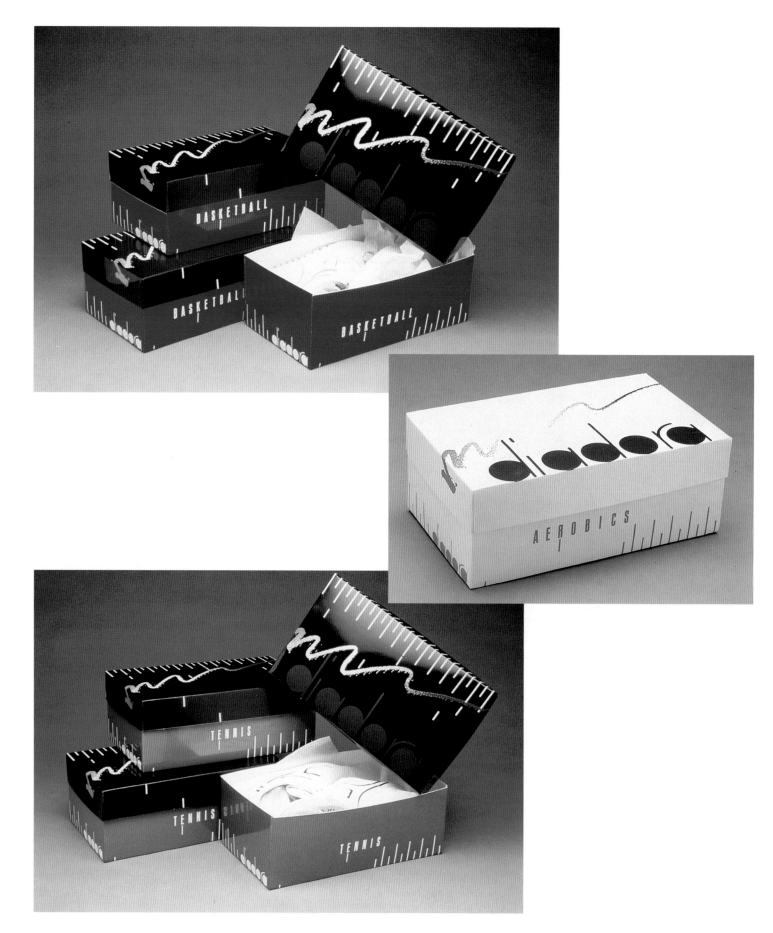

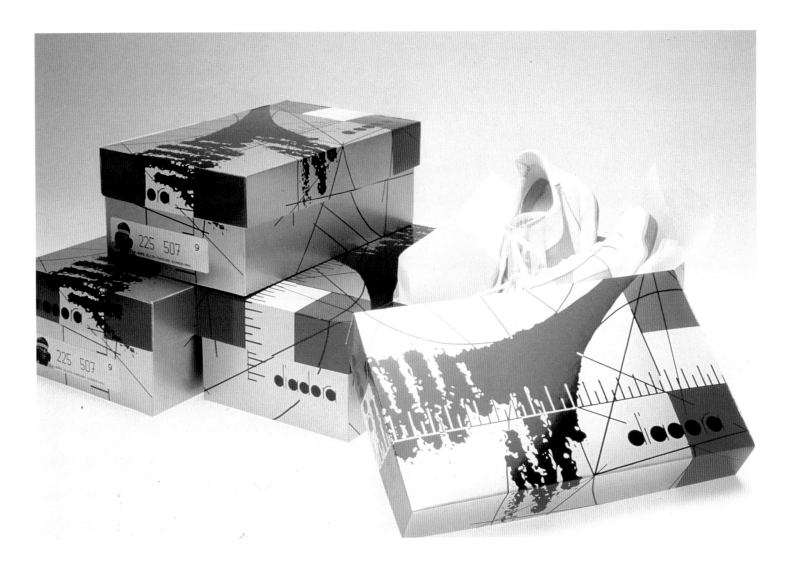

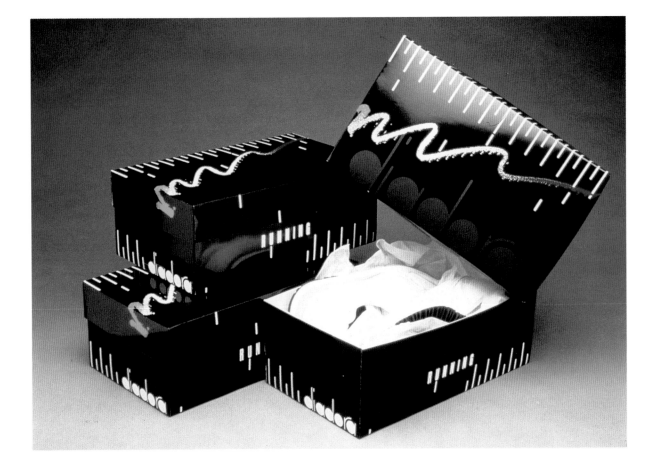

CAMEL CIGARETTE ADVERTISING

Task

Design a series of advertisements that would undo the image of the company's major competitor by resurrecting Camel's past reputation as the tough guy's cigarette of choice.

Design Strategies

The designer unearthed the characters with a penchant for smoking in their famous movie roles. Period illustration styles were employed, which evolved into the Joe Camel character. Ultimately, however, these designs were rejected in favor of another style.

Design Firm: Mike Salisbury
   Communications, Inc.
Client: R.J. Reynolds
Art Director and Designer: Mike Salisbury

INTEL MOBILE COMMUNICATOR PACKAGING

Task

Design a package similar to the family of Intel software packaging.

Design Strategies

Photography was used depicting a forest backdrop to emphasize the mobile, out-of-office setting that the product represented —staying in touch when you're on the road. The product design was well liked, but the project was put on indefinite hold and the packaging was never taken past the comp stage.

Design Firm: Hornall Anderson Design
    Works, Inc.
Client: Intel Corporation
Art Directors: Jack Anderson, Julia LaPine
Designers: Jack Anderson, Julia LaPine,
    Heidi Favour, Bruce Branson-Meyer

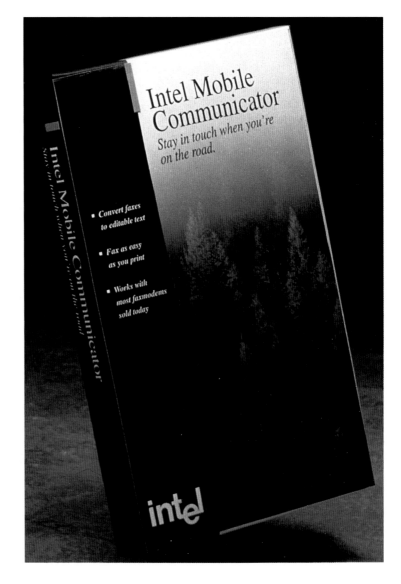

RETOOL LOGO

Task

Develop a symbol for a progressive firm that designs marketing tools and products based on the needs of the consumer.

Design Strategies

The challenge was to take a complex, modern idea and give it a simple, revolutionary look. The approach was to create masculine, rock-solid, stable marks that combined intriguing concepts with timeless elements. The designers used the gear—a universal symbol of work—to connote the idea of remaking the tools of marketing. Some submissions were redesigned to incorporate an eloquent style. Although the client liked the ideas, the company never got off the ground.

Design Firm: Planet Design Company
Client: Retool Corporation
Art Directors: Dana Lytle, Kevin Wade
Designers: Dana Lytle, Kevin Wade, Martha Graettinger

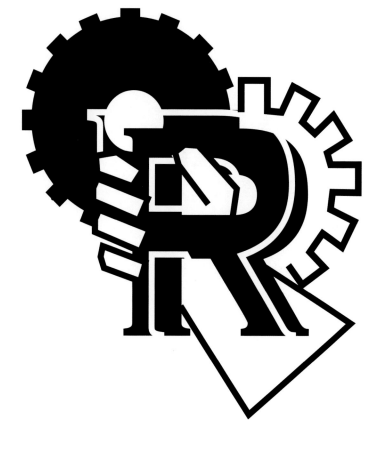

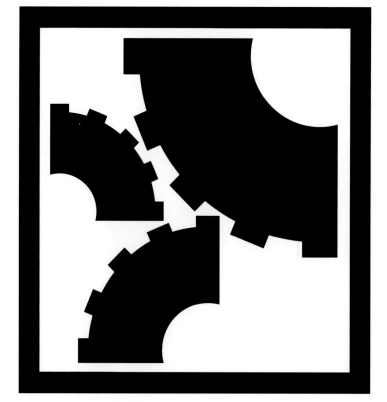

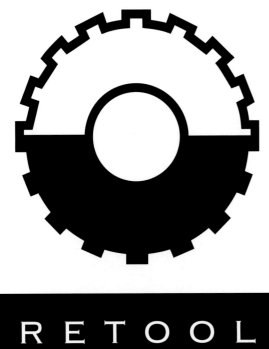

R E T O O L

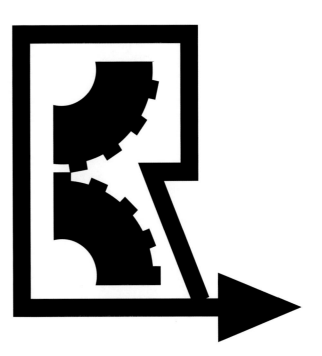

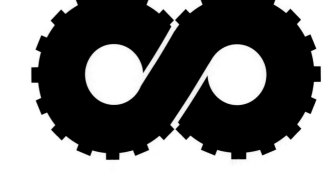

R E T O O L

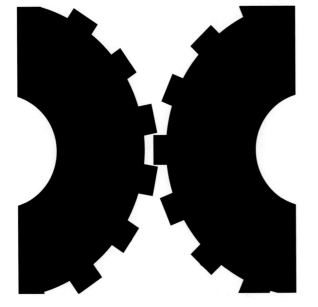

R E T O O L

R E T O O L   C O R P

MAKITA CAMPAIGN

Task

Design a campaign to sell the client's tools and new battery pack product.

Design Strategies

These solutions all attempt to demonstrate methods by which the client could reeducate the public as to the value of its products. The aesthetic copy direction was also the most preferred by the designer, featuring shots of the product as inserts and the lightning as a focused image. These solutions were all rejected, but may be reconsidered at another time.

Design Firm: Mike Salisbury
   Communications, Inc.
Client: Makita Tools
Art Director and Designer: Mike Salisbury
Illustrators: Pat Linse, Doyle Anderson,
   Scott Binkley
Photographer: Andrew Newhart

Super Mak Pak is here.

It's your paycheck so we took the time to get it right.

NOTHING CAN BEAT A MAKITA

makita

HE'S BIG.

HE'S BLUE.

HE'S PACKING

SERIOUS

FIREPOWER.

New! **Super MakPak**

The only high capacity battery system up to **MAKITA POWER**

Now the world's most powerful tools are 40% stronger and Makita's exclusive Power Display lets you see all that power.

Super MakPak. Serious firepower. from *makita*

SALAD TIME PACKAGING

Task

Redesign packaging on spec for a ready-to-eat salad mix for a local advertising agency.

Design Strategies

The designers created a window to frame the chopped lettuce, keeping the packaging elements organized into tight groupings that isolated the identity from the busy visual background and using dark border colors to heighten the contrast between the product and package. Because the pre-cut salad was a new product and more expensive than loose vegetables, they aimed the design at a more upscale market—a professional, health-conscious adult. The design with red borders was a refinement of the existing package; the final design was similar to this, except with a blue ruled frame rather than top and bottom borders, and was created by other designers.

Design Firm: Shields Design
Client: Salad Time
Art Director and Designer: Charles Shields

MIRADOR LOGO

Task

Create a logo for a new company that manufactures high quality, small quantity color computer printers.

Design Strategies

The general concept for both solutions was based on the meaning of the Spanish word mirador—a vantage point with an extensive view. An interpretation of a soaring bird looking downward was used to form the abstract letter "M." The designers developed a modern look with a minimal gestural approach and avoided specific references to technology. Varied line weight and spaced typography were used to achieve a spacious appearance while maintaining a strong association with the Spanish word. The client, however, later decided not to use the name "Mirador;" its parent company would instead design a logo in-house for the new company name, "Color Graphics."

Design Firm: Mortensen Design
Client: Stern Marketing Group/Xerox
Art Director: Gordon Mortensen
Designers: Gordon Mortensen, David Stuhr

WHITE SEAS LABEL

Task

Design a label for canned oysters for gourmet specialty shops as well as supermarkets.

Design Strategies

The supermarket application incorporated images of the sky and sea with colors that implied freshness. Graphic images contrasted well with competing labels. The labels designed for gourmet outlets used rich colors and gold accents to emphasize sophistication and elegance, and appeal to a clientele interested in quality. Variations of designs for both baby and whole oysters were selected by the client. While in production, however, the company discovered it was unable to meet the quantity demands required for marketing, and the project was terminated.

Design Firm: Neville Smith Graphic Design
Client: White Seas Inc.
Art Director, Designer, and Illustrator:
    Neville Smith

OLD GRINGO ADVERTISING

Task

Design advertising that would sell a period movie with a famous cast.

Design Strategies

The basic premise of most movie posters is to show the personalities and a hint of the story line, and add proper graphic positioning. The designer traveled to Argentina to create the looks that said "big"—big stars, big production—and some element to offset the nostalgia of the story line. That element became the contemporary photography. The final piece was not that of the designer, but was assembled from his ideas.

Design Firm: Mike Salisbury
   Communications, Inc.
Client: Tri-Star Pictures
Art Director and Designer: Mike Salisbury
Illustrators: Brian Sisson, Scott Binkley

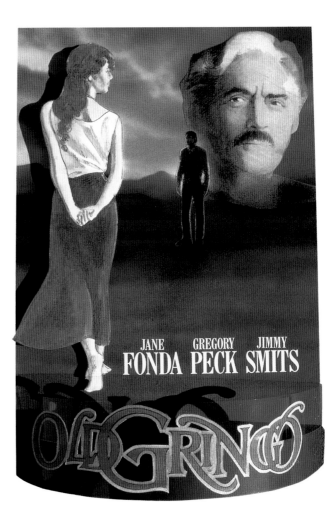

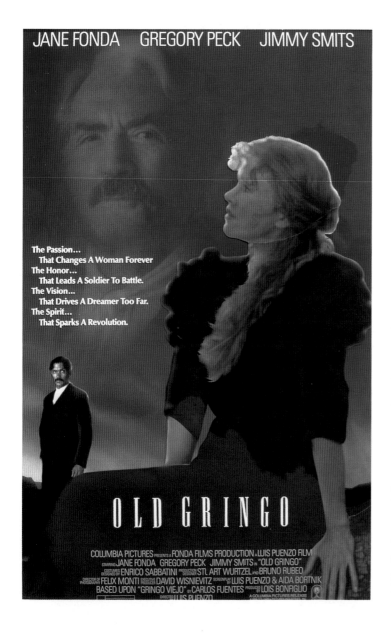

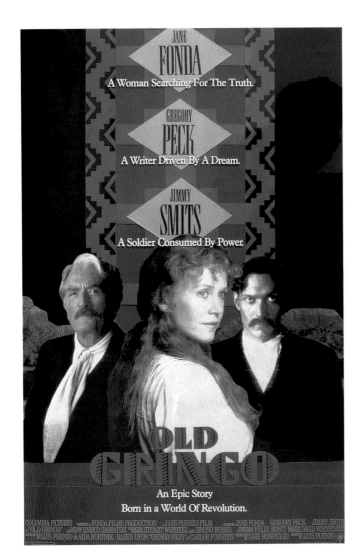

ODZ BOTKINS/
CAMP SUNSHINE
LOGO

Task

Design a logo/label for a line of children's clothing.

Design Strategies

A company that never got off the ground, "Odz Botkins" nonetheless provided the foundation for a second solution. A local children's hospital asked the studio to donate a T-shirt design for a summer camp for children with cancer. The "Odz Botkins" face was combined with clip art elements. But the final design, again, was not used.

Design Firm: Shields Design
Client: Odz Botkins
Art Director, Designer, and Illustrator:
   Charles Shields

CHANNEL SURFING PACKAGE DESIGN

Task

Create a package design for a game that used a remote control and television.

Design Strategies

With young adults as the target market, the designers created a "hip" character who "surfed" on a remote control. Colors were fun and attention-getting, and the type treatment, contemporary and unique. The funky look was achieved in the initial rounds, but readability was a problem. The final solution read well, and maintained a distinct identity. Unfortunately, focus group studies revealed that the target audience liked the package, but not the game. An older, more middle-American group liked the game, but not the package. Back to the drawing board...

Design Firm: John Evans Design
Client: Milton Bradley Company
Art Director: Jim Bremer
Designer and Illustrator: John Evans

HORSE AROUND BOOK SERIES

Task

Create a self-promotion that would show-case the designer's graphic, illustrative, and problem-solving skills.

Design Strategies

The designer created a series of seven books, each focusing on a different aspect of "the horse:" its history, mythology, build, and coloration, for instance. A staunch animal-lover, the designer originally used the set as a portfolio piece; later she tried unsuccessfully to sell the concept to publishers and paper mills.

Design Firm: Trudy Cole-Zielanski Design
Art Director, Designer, and Illustrator:
  Trudy Cole-Zielanski

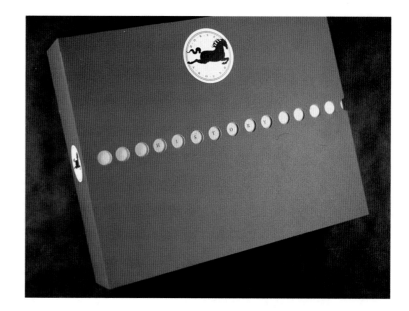

and our own wonderful imagination,the simple addition of a   creates...

PSYCHO II ADVERTISING CAMPAIGN

Task

Create a campaign to promote the sequel to the classic *Psycho* film, 20 years later.

Design Strategies

To relive the original terror of the first film, the designers used its well-known symbols, such as those of the mother and a shower, portrayed in a modern, compelling way. Unfortunately, another direction was undertaken and none of these submissions was accepted.

Design Firm: Mike Salisbury
    Communications, Inc.
Client: Universal
Art Director and Designer: Mike Salisbury
Illustrator: Terry Lamb

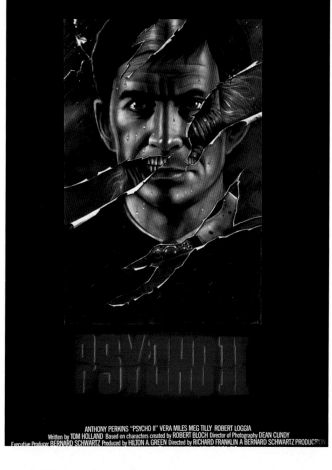

MARINA VILLAGE IDENTITY

Task

Design an identity for an upscale ethnic restaurant.

Design Strategies

The client was looking for an image that reflected both sophistication and a sense of uniqueness. The restaurant was based on the concept of providing the best of ethnic cuisine from all over the world in one central place. After the designs were submitted, the client decided to change the direction of the restaurant to one of fun and casual dining. Both designs, therefore, were rejected.

Design Firm: Design Objectives Pte Ltd
Client: Marina Village International
Art Director and Designer: Ronnie S.C. Tan

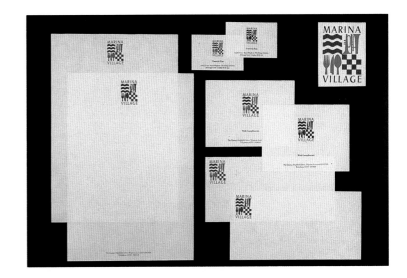

SPIRULINA LOGO

Task
Design a graphic identifier for a line of cosmetics that derive their benefit from a natural Hawaiian ingredient.

Design Strategies
The client requested a look that reflected Hawaii's tropical paradise and effectively supported typography. Floral and plant images were used with whimsical and flowing type for an appropriately lively look, while color added a refreshing appeal. The project never materialized, however.

Design Firm: Toni Schowalter Design
Client: La Parfumerie
Art Director: Toni Schowalter
Designers: Toni Schowalter, Ilene Price

SPIRULINA

EXPO POSTER

Task

Design a poster as part of a series based on a man, transportation, and communication theme.

Design Strategies

The graphic approach incorporated symbols of transportation and communication, such as motion, space travel, and communication satellites packaged in an envelope that represented the Canadian mail service.

Design Firm: Neville Smith Graphic Design
Client: Canadian Participation Expo
Art Director, Designer, and Illustrator:
   Neville Smith

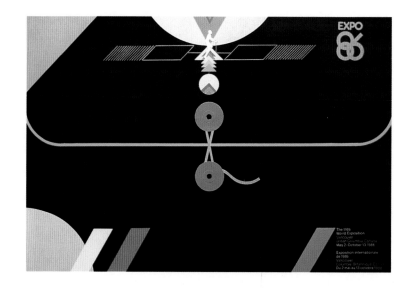

JAZZ POSTER

Task

Design a poster within one week for a jazz concert benefiting a youth organization.

Design Strategies

Due to an extremely tight timeframe, a very crude, loose pencil sketch approach not only solved the time problem, but also seemed to capture the impromptu feeling associated with jazz. The client liked it, but, unfortunately, had something a little glitzier in mind, which was produced by someone else.

Design Firm: John Evans Design
Client: Rainbow Bridge
Art Director, Designer, and Illustrator: John Evans

CROWN PRINTING PRESENTATION FOLDER

Task

Design a presentation folder to support the company's new identity.

Design Strategies

The logo, which was created by Shields Design, used a 4-color process illustration of a gold coin with a crown sculpted on it. The printed images using the color logo were so brilliant, the designers decided to downplay the folder's color so that when the folder was opened, the more brilliant images would be revealed. The intention was to print a quadtone version of the logo positioned on gold lamé cloth. Unfortunately, the client opted to print only a few identity materials, and the presentation folder was dropped.

Design Firm: Shields Design
Client: Crown Printing
Art Director, Designer, and Illustrator:
  Charles Shields

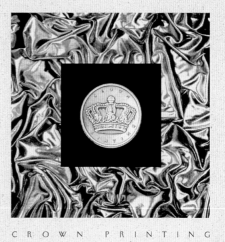

CROWN PRINTING

CROWN

PRINTING

Jenny A. Dowdy
SALES REPRESENTATIVE

1730 "H" Street
Fresno, California 93721
209-233-4177
FAX: 209-233-7473

LUCAS ANNUAL REPORT

Task

Create a concept proposal for the front cover of the client's annual report.

Design Strategies

To heighten awareness of the client's capabilities in developing high technology systems for the automotive and aerospace industries, the designers featured the revolutionary Osprey tilt-rotor aircraft, which can fly vertically or horizontally thanks to the client's actuation system. By pulling a tab at the side of the piece, the aircraft's "engines" rotate 90 degrees as if the pilot was changing flight mode from vertical to horizontal. An innovative concept, but it was rejected.

Design Firm: Tor Pettersen & Partners Ltd
Client: Lucas Industries PLC
Art Director: Tor Pettersen
Designer: Jeff Davis
Illustrator: Colin Frewin

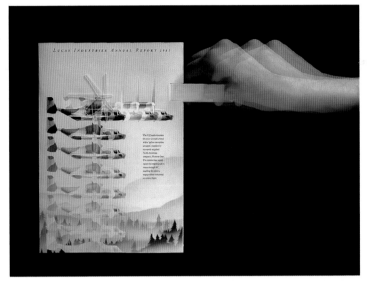

WEARHOUSE SPORTSWEAR

Task

Design visual identities for merchandise that represents a well-attended sports event.

Design Strategies

The designers portrayed a wide range of sportswear applications, using styles from illustrative to contemporary. Colors were consistently bright, and designs were created to be visible from a distance, while still being attractive enough to wear anywhere. Unfortunately, although the client was impressed with these designs, the project was put on hold indefinitely shortly after the work was completed.

Design Firm: Supon Design Group
Client: Wearhouse
Art Director: Andrew Dolan
Designers: Maria Sese Paul,
    Apisak "Eddie" Saibua

LONDON DESIGN CORPORATE IDENTITY

Task
Create or restyle an identity so that it reflects a corporation's changing direction.

Design Strategies
To accurately depict the progressive objectives of the firm, the design called for a powerful, vibrant image. The designers emphasized bright colors and strong lines so that the designs would remain striking, regardless of application. Although the client liked the new designs, concern later developed that they may not match the success of the old logo, and the client eventually opted not to proceed with the change.

Design Firm: Design Objectives Pte Ltd.
Client: London Design System (S) Pte Ltd.
Art Director and Designer: Ronnie S.C. Tan

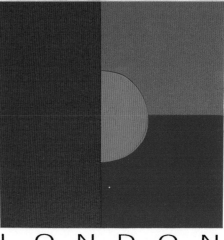

STARBUCKS CONFECTIONS PACKAGING

Task

Design packaging for a line of retail specialty products that was different from the traditional four-sided box.

Design Strategies

The box configuration went through several stages before the final design was chosen. One constant, however, was the use of a window through which the product could show. The background color grew deeper and bolder; and a three-sided box was presented, then stopped at the mechanical stage. It was believed that such a format was too representative of a gift-like product. Ultimately, the packaging was designed to resemble that of snack packaging in order to encourage more impulse purchases.

Design Firm: Hornall Anderson Design Works, Inc.
Client: Starbucks Coffee Company
Art Director: Jack Anderson
Designers: Jack Anderson, Julie Lock
Illustrator: Julia LaPine

DESIGN FIRM INDEX

CLIENT INDEX